TEXTBOOK EDITION

∴

# THE CHRONICLES
# OF AMERICA SERIES
## ALLEN JOHNSON
### EDITOR

GERHARD R. LOMER
CHARLES W. JEFFERYS
ASSISTANT EDITORS

SECRETARY SEWARD      EDWARD STOECKEL,      CHARLES SUMNER
                      Russian Minister

SIGNING THE TREATY FOR THE PURCHASE OF ALASKA

# THE
# PATH OF EMPIRE

### A CHRONICLE OF THE
### UNITED STATES AS A WORLD POWER
### BY CARL RUSSELL FISH

NEW HAVEN: YALE UNIVERSITY PRESS
TORONTO: GLASGOW, BROOK & CO.
LONDON: HUMPHREY MILFORD
OXFORD UNIVERSITY PRESS

1921

# CONTENTS

vii

# ILLUSTRATION

# THE PATH OF EMPIRE

.·.

## CHAPTER I

### THE MONROE DOCTRINE

In 1815 the world found peace after twenty-two years of continual war. In the forests of Canada and the pampas of South America, throughout all the countries of Europe, over the plains of Russia and the hills of Palestine, men and women had known what war was and had prayed that its horrors might never return. In even the most autocratic states subjects and rulers were for once of one mind: in the future war must be prevented. To secure peace forever was the earnest desire of two statesmen so strongly contrasted as the impressionable Czar Alexander I of Russia, acclaimed as the "White Angel" and the "Universal Savior," and Prince Metternich, the real ruler of Austria, the spider who was for the next thirty years to spin the web of European secret diplomacy. While the Czar invited all governments to unite in a "Holy Alliance" to prevent war, Metternich for the same purpose formed the less holy but more powerful "Quadruple Alliance" of Russia, Prussia, Austria, and England.

The designs of Metternich, however, went far beyond the mere prevention of war. To his mind the cause of all the upheavals which had convulsed Europe was the spirit of liberty bred in France in the days of the Revolution; if order was to be restored, there must be a return to the former autocratic principle of government, to the doctrine of "Divine Right"; it was for kings and emperors to command; it was the duty of subjects to obey. These principles had not, it was true, preserved peace in the past, but Metternich now proposed that, in the future, sovereigns or their representatives should meet "at fixed periods" to adjust their own differences and to assist one another in enforcing the obedience of subjects everywhere. The rulers were reasonably well satisfied with the world as it was arranged by the Congress of Vienna in 1815 and determined to set their faces against any change in the relations of governments to one another or to their subjects. They regretted, indeed, that the Government of the United States was built upon the sands of a popular vote, but they recognized that it was apparently well established and decently respectable, and therefore worthy of recognition by the mutual protection society of the Holy Alliance.

The subjects of these sovereigns, however, did not all share the satisfaction of their masters, and some of them soon showed that much as they desired peace they desired other things even more. The inhabitants of Spanish America, while their imperial mother was in the chaos of Napoleon's wars, had nibbled at the forbidden fruit of freedom. They particularly desired freedom to buy the products of British factories, which cost less and satisfied better than those previously furnished by the Spanish merchants, secure in their absolute monopoly. With peace came renewed monopoly, haughty officials, and oppressive laws dictated by that most stupid of the restored sovereigns, Ferdinand VII of Spain. Buenos Aires, however, never recognized his rule, and her general, the knightly San Martín, in one of the most remarkable campaigns of history, scaled the Andes and carried the flag of revolution into Chili and Peru. Venezuela, that hive of revolution, sent forth Bolívar to found the new republics of

Colombia and Bolivia. Mexico freed herself, and Brazil separated herself from Portugal. By 1822 European rule had been practically swept off the American mainland, from Cape Horn to the borders of Canada, and, except for the empire of Dom Pedro in Brazil, the newly born nations had adopted the republican form of government which the European monarchs despised. The spirit of unrest leaped eastward across the Atlantic. Revolutions in Spain, Portugal, and Naples sought impiously and with constitutions to bind the hands of their kings. Even the distant Greeks and Serbians sought their independence from the Turk.

Divine Right, just rescued from the French Revolution, was tottering and had yet to test the strength of its new props, the "Holy" and the "Quadruple" alliances, and the policy of intervention to maintain the *status quo*. Congresses at Aix-la-Chapelle in 1818, at Troppau in 1820, and at Laibach in 1821, decided to refuse recognition to governments resting on such revolutions, to offer mediation to restore the old order, and, if this were refused, to intervene by force. In the United States, on the other hand, founded on the right of revolution and dedicated to government by the people, these popular movements were greeted with enthusiasm. The fiery Clay, speaker and leader of the House of Representatives, made himself champion of the cause of the Spanish Americans; Daniel Webster thundered forth the sympathy of all lovers of antiquity for the Greeks; and Samuel Gridley Howe, an impetuous young American doctor, crossed the seas, carrying to the Greeks his services and the gifts of Boston friends of liberty. A new conflict seemed to be shaping itself — a struggle of absolutism against democracy, of America against Europe.

Between the two camps, both in her ideas and in her geographical situation, stood England. Devoted as she was to law and order, bulwark against the excesses of the French Terror and the world dominion that Napoleon sought, she was nevertheless equally strong in her opposition to Divine Right. Her people and her government alike were troubled at the repressive measures by which the Allies put down the Revolution of Naples in 1821 and that of Spain in 1823. Still more were they disturbed at the hint given at the Congress of Verona in 1822 that, when Europe was once quieted, America would engage the attention of Europe's arbiters. George Canning, the English foreign minister, soon discovered that this hint foreshadowed

a new congress to be devoted especially to the
American problem. Spain was to be restored to
her sovereignty, but was to pay in liberal grants of
American territory to whatever powers helped her.
Canning is regarded as the ablest English foreign
minister of the nineteenth century; at least no one
better embodied the fundamental aspirations of
the English people. He realized that liberal England would be perpetually a minority in a united
Europe, as Europe was then organized. He believed that the best security for peace was not a
union but a balance of powers. He opposed intervention in the internal affairs of nations and stood
for the right of each to choose its own form of
government. Particularly he fixed his eyes on
America, where he hoped to find weight to help him
balance the autocrats of the Old World. He wished
to see the new American republics free, and he believed that in freedom of trade England would obtain from them all that she needed. Alarmed at
the impending European intervention to restore
the rule of Spain or of her monarchical assignees
in America, he sought an understanding with the
United States. He proposed to Richard Rush, the
United States minister in London, that the two countries declare concurrently that the independence

of Spanish America was a fact, that the recognition of the new governments was a matter of time and circumstance, that neither country desired any portion of Spain's former dominions, but that neither would look with indifference upon the transfer of any portion of them to another power.

On October 9, 1823, this proposal reached Washington. The answer would be framed by able and most experienced statesmen. The President, James Monroe, had been almost continuously in public service since 1782. He had been minister to France, Spain, and England, and had been Secretary of State. In his earlier missions he had often shown an unwise impetuosity and an independent judgment which was not always well balanced. He had, however, grown in wisdom. He inspired respect by his sterling qualities of character, and he was an admirable presiding officer. William H. Crawford, his Secretary of the Treasury, John C. Calhoun, his Secretary of War, William Wirt, his Attorney-General, and even John McLean, his Postmaster-General, not then a member of the Cabinet, were all men who were considered as of presidential caliber.

Foremost in ability and influence, however, was John Quincy Adams, the Secretary of State.

Brought up from early boyhood in the atmosphere
of diplomacy, familiar with nearly every country of
Europe, he had nevertheless none of those arts of
suavity which are popularly associated with the
diplomat. Short, bald-headed, with watery eyes,
he on the one hand repelled familiarity, and on the
other hand shocked some sensibilities, as for example when he appeared in midsummer Washington without a neckcloth. His early morning swim
in the Potomac and his translations of Horace did
not conquer a temper which embittered many who
had business with him, while the nightly records
which he made of his interviews show that he was
generally suspicious of his visitors. Yet no American can show so long a roll of diplomatic successes.
Preëminently he knew his business. His intense devotion and his native talent had made him a master of the theory and practice of international law
and of statecraft. Always he was obviously honest,
and his word was relied on. Fundamentally he was
kind, and his work was permeated by a generous
enthusiasm. Probably no man in America had so
intense a conviction not only of the correctness
of American principles and the promise of American greatness but of the immediate strength and
greatness of the United States as it stood in 1823.

Fully aware as Adams was of the danger that threatened both America and liberty, he was not in favor of accepting Canning's proposal for the co-operation of England and the United States. He based his opposition upon two fundamental objections. In the first place he was not prepared to say that the United States desired no more Spanish territory. Not that Adams desired or would tolerate conquest. At the time of the Louisiana Purchase he had wished to postpone annexation until the assent of the people of that province could be obtained. But he believed that all the territory necessary for the geographical completeness of the United States had not yet been brought under the flag. He had just obtained Florida from Spain and a claim westward to the Pacific north of the forty-second parallel, but he considered the Southwest — Texas, New Mexico, and California — a natural field of expansion. These areas, then almost barren of white settlers, he expected time to bring into the United States, and he also expected that the people of Cuba would ultimately rejoice to become incorporated in the Union. He wished natural forces to work out their own results, without let or hindrance.

Not only was Adams opposed to Canning's proposed self-denying ordinance, but he was equally averse to becoming a partner with England. Such coöperation might well prove in time to be an "entangling alliance," involving the United States in problems of no immediate concern to its people and certainly in a partnership in which the other member would be dominant. If Canning saw liberal England as a perpetual minority in absolutist Europe, Adams saw republican America as a perpetual inferior to monarchical England. Although England, with Canada, the West Indies, and her commerce, was a great American power, Adams believed that the United States, the oldest independent nation in America, with a government which gave the model to the rest, could not admit her to joint leadership, for her power was in, not of, America, and her government was monarchical. Already Adams had won a strategic advantage over Canning, for in the previous year, 1822, the United States had recognized the new South American republics.

Great as were the dangers involved in coöperation with England, however, they seemed to many persons of little moment compared with the menace of absolutist armies and navies in the New World or of, perhaps, a French Cuba and a Russian Mexico. The only effective obstacle to such

foreign intervention was the British Navy. Both
President Monroe and Thomas Jefferson, who in
his retirement was still consulted on all matters of
high moment, therefore favored the acceptance of
Canning's proposal as a means of detaching England from the rest of Europe. Adams argued,
however, that England was already detached; that,
for England's purposes, the British Navy would
still stand between Europe and America, whatever
the attitude of the United States; that compromise or concession was unnecessary; and that the
country could as safely take its stand toward the
whole outside world as toward continental Europe
alone. To reject the offer of a country whose assistance was absolutely necessary to the safety of
the United States, and to declare the American case
against her as well as against the more menacing
forces whose attack she alone could prevent, required a nerve and poise which could come only
from ignorant foolhardiness or from absolute knowledge of the facts. The self-assurance of Adams
was well founded, and no general on the field of
battle ever exhibited higher courage.

Adams won over the Cabinet, and the President
decided to incorporate in his annual message to Congress a declaration setting forth the attitude of the

United States toward all the world, and in particular denying the right of any European power, England included, to intervene in American affairs. In making such a statement, however, it was necessary to offer compensation in some form. The United States was not prepared to offer Canning's self-denying ordinance barring the way to further American expansion, but something it must offer. This compensating offset Adams found in the separation of the New World from the Old and in abstention from interference in Europe. Such a renunciation involved, however, the sacrifice of generous American sympathies with the republicans across the seas. Monroe, Gallatin, and many other statesmen wished as active a policy in support of the Greeks as of the Spanish Americans. Adams insisted, however, that the United States should create a sphere for its interests and should confine itself to that sphere. His plan for peace provided that European and American interests should not only not clash but should not even meet.

The President's message of December 2, 1823, amounted to a rejection of the Holy Alliance as guardian of the world's peace, of Canning's request for an *entente*, and of the proposal that the United States enter upon a campaign to republicanize the world. It stated the intention of the Government to refrain from interference in Europe, and its belief that it was "impossible that the allied powers should extend their political system to any portion of either continent [of America] without endangering our peace and happiness." The message contained a strong defense of the republican system of government and of the right of nations to control their own internal development. It completed the foreign policy of the United States by declaring, in connection with certain recent encroachments of Russia along the northwest coast, that the era of colonization in the Americas was over. The United States was to maintain in the future that boundaries between nations holding land in America actually existed and could be traced — a position which invited arbitration in place of force.

Both Canning and Adams won victories, but neither realized his full hopes. Canning prevented the interference of Europe in Spanish America, broke up the Quadruple Alliance, rendered the Holy Alliance a shadow, and restored a balance of power that meant safety for England for almost a hundred years; but he failed to dictate American policy. Adams on his part detached the United States from European politics without throwing

England into the arms of Europe. He took advan
tage of the divisions of the Old World to establish the
priority of the United States in American affairs
but he failed in his later attempt to unite all the
Americas in cordial coöperation. Earnest as wa
his desire and hard as he strove in 1825 when he
had become President with Clay as his Secretary
of State, Adams found that the differences in poin
of view between the United States and the othe
American powers were too great to permit a Pan
American policy. The Panama Congress on which
he built his hopes failed, and for fifty years th
project lay dormant.

Under the popular name of the Monroe Doc
trine, however, Adams's policy has played a much
larger part in world affairs than he expected
Without the force of law either in this country o
between nations, this doctrine took a firm hold o
the American imagination and became a nationa
ideal, while other nations have at least in form
taken cognizance of it. The Monroe Doctrine ha
survived because Adams did not invent its main
tenets but found them the dominating principles o
American international politics; his work, like tha
of his contemporary John Marshall, was one of codi
fication. But not all those who have commented

on the work of Adams have possessed his ana-
lytical mind, and many have confused what was
fundamental in his pronouncement with what was
temporary and demanded by the emergency of
the time.

Always the American people have stood, from
the first days of their migration to America, for the
right of the people of a territory to determine their
own development. First they have insisted that
their own right to work out their political destiny
be acknowledged and made safe. For this they
fought the Revolution. It has followed that they
have in foreign affairs tried to keep their hands free
from entanglements with other countries and have
refrained from interference with foreign politics.
This was the burden of Washington's *Farewell
Address*, and it was a message which Jefferson re-
iterated in his inaugural. These are the permanent principles which have controlled enlightened
American statesmen in their attitude toward the
world, from the days of John Winthrop to those of
Woodrow Wilson.

It was early found, however, that the affairs of
the immediate neighbors of the United States
continually and from day to day affected the
whole texture of American life and that actually

they limited American independence and therefore could not be left out of the policy of the Government. The United States soon began to recognize that there was a region in the affairs of which it must take a more active interest. As early as 1780 Thomas Pownall, an English colonial official, predicted that the United States must take an active part in Cuban affairs. In 1806 Madison, then Secretary of State, had instructed Monroe, Minister to Great Britain, that the Government began to broach the idea that the whole Gulf Stream was within its maritime jurisdiction. The message of Monroe was an assertion that the fate of both the Americas was of immediate concern to the safety of the United States, because the fate of its sister republics intimately affected its own security. This proved to be an enduring definition of policy, because for many years there was a real institutional difference between the American hemisphere and the rest of the world and because oceanic boundaries were the most substantial that the world affords.

Adams, however, would have been the last to claim that his method of securing the fundamental purposes of the United States was itself fundamental. It is particularly important for Americans to make a distinction between the things which they have always wished to obtain and the methods which they have from time to time used. To build a policy today on the alleged isolation of the American continents would be almost as absurd as to try to build a government on the belief in Divine Right. The American continents are no longer separated from the rest of the world by their national institutions, because the spirit of these institutions has permeated much of Europe, Asia, and even Africa. No boundaries, not even oceans, can today prohibit international interference. But while the particular method followed in 1823 is no longer appropriate, the ends which the United States set out to attain have remained the same. Independence, absolute and complete, including the absence of all entanglements which might draw the country into other peoples' quarrels; the recognition of a similar independence in all other peoples, which involves both keeping its own hands off and also strongly disapproving of interference by one nation with another — these have been the guiding principles of the United States. These principles the Government has maintained by such means as seemed appropriate to the time. In colonial days the people of America fought in courts for their charter rights; at the time of the

2

Revolution, by arms for their independence from England; during the Napoleonic wars, for their independence from the whole system of Europe. The Monroe Doctrine declared that to maintain American independence from the European system it was necessary that the European system be excluded from the Americas. In entering the Great War in the twentieth century the United States has recognized that the system of autocracy against which Monroe fulminated must disappear from the entire world if, under modern industrial conditions, real independence is to exist anywhere.

It is the purpose of the following chapters to trace the expansion of American interests in the light of the Monroe Doctrine and to explain those controversies which accompanied this growth and taxed the diplomatic resources of American Secretaries of State from the times of Adams and Webster and Seward to those of Blaine and Hay and Elihu Root. The diplomacy of the Great War is reserved for another volume in this Series.

# CHAPTER II

## CONTROVERSIES WITH GREAT BRITAIN

No two nations have ever had more intimate relationships than the United States and Great Britain. Speaking the same language and owning a common racial origin in large part, they have traded with each other and in the same regions, and geographically their territories touch for three thousand miles. During the nineteenth century the coastwise shipping of the United States was often forced to seek the shelter of the British West Indies. The fisherfolk of England and America mingled on the Grand Bank of Newfoundland and on the barren shores of that island and of Labrador, where they dried their fish. Indians, criminals, and game crossed the Canadian boundary at will, streams flowed across it, and the coast cities vied for the trade of the interior, indifferent to the claims of national allegiance. One cannot but believe that this intimacy has in the long run made for friendship and peace; but it has also meant constant controversy, often pressed to the verge of war by the pertinacious insistence of both nations on their full rights as they saw them.

The fifteen years following Adams's encounter with Canning saw the gradual accumulation of a number of such disputes, which made the situation in 1840 exceptionally critical. Great Britain was angered at the failure of the United States to grant her the right to police the seas for the suppression of the slave trade, while the United States, with memories of the vicious English practice of impressment before the War of 1812, distrusted the motives of Great Britain in asking for this right. Nearly every mile of the joint boundary in North America was in dispute, owing to the vagueness of treaty descriptions or to the errors of surveyors. Twelve thousand square miles and a costly American fort were involved; arbitration had failed; rival camps of lumberjacks daily imperiled peace; and both the Maine Legislature and the National Congress had voted money for defense. In a New York jail Alexander McLeod was awaiting trial in a state court for the murder of an American on the steamer *Caroline*, which a party of Canadian militia had cut out from the American shore near Buffalo and had sent to destruction over Niagara Falls. The British Government, holding that the *Caroline* was at the time illegally employed to assist Canadian insurgents, and that the Canadian militia were under government orders justifiable by international law, assumed the responsibility for McLeod's act and his safety. Ten thousand Americans along the border, members of "Hunters' Lodges," were anxious for a war which would unleash them for the conquest of Canada. Delay was causing all these disputes to fester, and the public mind of the two countries was infected with hostility.

Fortunately in 1841 new administrations came into power in both England and the United States. Neither the English Tories nor the American Whigs felt bound to maintain all the contentions of their predecessors, and both desired to come to an agreement. The responsibility on the American side fell upon Daniel Webster, the new Secretary of State. With less foreign experience than John Quincy Adams, he was more a man of the world and a man among men. His conversation was decidedly less ponderous than his oratory, and there was no more desirable dinner guest in America. Even in Webster's lightest moments, his majestic head gave the impression of colossal mentality, and his eyes, when he was in earnest, almost hypnotized those upon whom he bent his gaze. A leading figure in public life for twenty-five years, he now attained administrative position for the first time, and his constant practice at the bar had given something of a lawyer-like trend to his mind.

The desire of the British Government for an agreement with the United States was shown by the selection of Washington instead of London as the place of negotiation and of Lord Ashburton as negotiator. The head of the great banking house of Baring Brothers, he had won his title by service and was, moreover, known to be a friend of the United States. While in Philadelphia in his youth, he had married Miss Bingham of that city, and she still had American interests. In the controversies before the War of 1812 Lord Ashburton had supported many of the American contentions. He knew Webster personally, and they both looked forward to the social pleasure of meeting again during the negotiations. The two representatives came together in this pleasant frame of mind and did most of their business at the dinner table, where it is reported that more than diplomatic conversation flowed. They avoided an exchange of notes, which would bind each to a position once taken, but first came to an agreement and then prepared the documents.

It must not be supposed, however, that either Ashburton or Webster sacrificed the claims of his own Government. Webster certainly was a good attorney for the United States in settling the boundary disputes, as is shown by the battle of the maps. The territorial contentions of both countries hung largely upon the interpretation of certain clauses of the first American treaty of peace. Webster therefore ordered a search for material to be made in the archives of Paris and London. In Paris there was brought to light a map with the boundary drawn in red, possibly by Franklin, and supporting the British contention. Webster refrained from showing this to Ashburton and ordered search in London discontinued. Ironically enough, however, a little later there was unearthed in the British Museum the actual map used by one of the British commissioners in 1782, which showed the boundary as the United States claimed it to be. Though they had been found too late to affect the negotiations, these maps disturbed the Senate discussion of the matter. Yet, as they offset each other, they perhaps facilitated the acceptance of the treaty.

Rapidly Webster and Ashburton cleared the field. Webster obtained the release of McLeod and effected the passage of a law to prevent a similar crisis in the future by permitting such cases to be transferred to a federal court. The *Caroline* affair was settled by an amicable exchange of notes in which each side conceded much to the other. They did not indeed dispose of the slave trade, but they reached an agreement by which a joint squadron was to undertake to police efficiently the African seas in order to prevent American vessels from engaging in that trade.

Upon the more important matter of boundary, both Webster and Ashburton decided to give up the futile task of convincing each other as to the meaning of phrases which rested upon half-known facts reaching back into the misty period of first discovery and settlement. They abandoned interpretation and made compromise and division the basis of their settlement. This method was more difficult for Webster than for Ashburton, as both Maine and Massachusetts were concerned, and each must under the Constitution be separately convinced. Here Webster used the "Red Line" map, and succeeded in securing the consent of these States. They finally settled upon a boundary which was certainly not that intended in 1782 but was a compromise between the two conceptions of that boundary and divided the territory with a regard for actual conditions and geography. From Passamaquoddy Bay to the Lake of the Woods, accepted lines were substituted for controversy, and the basis of peace was thus made more secure. The treaty also contained provision for the mutual extradition of criminals guilty of specified crimes, but these did not include embezzlement, and "gone to Canada" was for years the epitaph of many a dishonest American who had been found out.

The friendly spirit in which Webster and Ashburton had carried on their negotiations inaugurated a period of reasonable amity between their two nations. The United States annexed Texas without serious protest; in spite of the clamor for "fifty-four forty or fight," Oregon was divided peacefully; and England did not take advantage of the war with Mexico. Each of these events, however, added to American territory, and these additions gave prominence to a new and vexing problem. The United States was now planted solidly upon the Pacific, and its borders were practically those to which Adams had looked forward. Natural and unified as this area looks upon the map and actually is today, in 1850 the extent of territorial expansion had overreached the means of transportation. The Great Plains, then regarded as the Great American Desert, and the Rockies presented impossible barriers to all but adventurous individuals. These men, uniting in bands for self-protection and taking their lives in their hands, were able with good luck to take themselves but little else across this central region and the western barrier. All ordinary communication, all mail and all freight, must go by sea. The United States was actually divided into two very unequal parts, and California and Oregon were geographically far distant colonies.

The ocean highroad belonged to the United States in common with all nations, but it took American ships to the opposite ends of the earth. No regular shuttle of traffic sufficient to weave the nation together could be expected to pass Cape Horn at every throw. The natural route lay obviously through the Caribbean, across some one of the isthmuses, and up the Pacific coast. Here, however, the United States would have to use territory belonging to other nations, and to obtain the right of transit and security agreement was necessary.

All these isthmus routes, moreover, needed improvement. Capital must be induced to do the work, and one necessary inducement was a guarantee of stable conditions of investment.

This isthmus route became for a time the prime object of American diplomacy. The United States made in 1846 satisfactory arrangements with the Republic of New Granada (later Colombia), across which lay the most southern route, and in 1853 with Mexico, of whose northern or Tehuantepec route many had great expectations; but a further difficulty was now discovered. The best lanes were those of Panama and of Nicaragua. When the discovery of gold in California in 1848 made haste a more important element in the problem, " Commodore " Vanderbilt, at that time the shipping king of the United States, devoted his attention to the Nicaragua route and made it the more popular. Here, however, the United States encountered not only the local independent authorities but also Great Britain. Just to the north of the proposed route Great Britain possessed Belize, now British Honduras, a meager colony but with elastic boundaries. For many generations, too, she had concerned herself with securing the rights of the Mosquito Indians, who held a territory, also with elastic boundaries, inconveniently near the San Juan River, the Caribbean entrance to the Nicaraguan thoroughfare. From Great Britain, moreover, must come a large portion of the capital to be employed in constructing the canal which was expected soon to cut the isthmus.

The local situation soon became acute. Costa Rica, Nicaragua, and the Mosquitoes all claimed the mouth of the San Juan; Honduras and Nicaragua, the control of the Pacific outlet. British diplomatic and naval officers clashed with those of the United States until, in their search for complete control, both exceeded the instructions which they had received from home. The British occupied Greytown on the San Juan and supported the Mosquitoes and Costa Rica. The Americans won favor in Nicaragua and Honduras, framed treaties allowing transit and canal construction, and proposed the annexation of Tigre Island, which commanded the proposed Pacific outlet.

To untie these knots, Sir Henry Bulwer was sent to Washington to negotiate with John M. Clayton, President Taylor's Secretary of State. Neither of these negotiators was of the caliber of Webster and Ashburton, and the treaty which they drew up proved rather a Pandora's box of future difficulties than a satisfactory settlement. In the first place it was agreed that any canal to be constructed over any of the isthmuses was to be absolutely neutral, in time of war as well as of peace. Both nations were to guarantee this neutrality, and other nations were invited to join with them. No other nations did join, however, and the project became a dual affair which, owing to the superiority of the British Navy, gave Britain the advantage, or would eventually have done so if a canal had been constructed. Subsequently the majority of Americans decided that such a canal must be under the sole control of the United States, and the treaty then stood as a stumbling block in the way of the realization of this idea.

More immediately important, however, and a great wrench to American policies, was the provision that neither power "will ever erect or maintain any fortifications commanding" the canal "or occupy, or fortify, or colonize, or assume or exercise any dominion over . . . any part of Central America." This condition violated Adams's principle that the United States was not on the same footing with any European power in American affairs and should not be bound by any self-denying ordinance, and actually it reversed the principle against the

United States. An explanatory note accompanying the treaty recognized that this provision did not apply to Belize and her dependencies, and Great Britain promptly denied that it applied to any rights she already possessed in Central America, including the Mosquito protectorate and certain Bay Islands which were claimed by Great Britain as dependencies of Belize and by Honduras as a part of her territory.

In vain did Webster, who succeeded Clayton, seek an agreement. His term of office passed, and the controversy fell into the hands of Lord Palmerston, the jingoistic spirit who began at this time to dominate British foreign policy, and of James Buchanan, who, known to us as a spineless seeker after peace where there was no peace, was at this time riding into national leadership on a wave of expansionist enthusiasm. Buchanan and Palmerston mutually shook the stage thunder of verbal extravagance, but probably neither intended war. Poker was at this time the national American game, and bluff was a highly developed art. The American player won a partial victory. In 1856 Great Britain agreed to withdraw her protectorate over the Mosquitoes, to acknowledge the supremacy of Honduras over the Bay Islands, and to accept a reasonable interpretation of the Belize boundary. Though this convention was never ratified, Great Britain carried out its terms, and in 1860 Buchanan announced himself satisfied.

The dreams of 1850, however, were not satisfied. A railroad was completed across Panama in 1855, but no canal was constructed until years after the great transcontinental railroads had bound California to the East by bonds which required no foreign sanction. Yet the Clayton-Bulwer Treaty remained an entangling alliance, destined to give lovers of peace and amity many more uncomfortable hours.

During the Civil War other causes of irritation arose between the United States and Great Britain. The proclamation of neutrality, by which the British Government recognized the Confederacy as a belligerent, seemed to the North an unfriendly act. Early in the war occurred the *Trent* affair, which added to the growing resentment.[1] It was held to be a violation of professed neutrality that Confederate commerce destroyers were permitted to be built and fitted out in British yards. The subsequent transfer of hundreds of thousands of

[1] See Stephenson, *Abraham Lincoln and the Union*, in *The Chronicles of America.*

tons of American shipping to British registry, owing to the depredations of these raiders, still further incensed the American people. (It was in the midst of these strained relations that the Fenian Brotherhood in the United States attempted the invasion of Canada.

America laid claims against Great Britain, based not merely on the actual destruction of merchantmen by the *Alabama*, the *Florida*, and other Confederate vessels built in British yards, but also on such indirect losses as insurance, cost of pursuit, and commercial profits. The American Minister, Charles Francis Adams, had proposed the arbitration of these claims, but the British Ministry declined to arbitrate matters involving the honor of the country. Adams's successor, Reverdy Johnson, succeeded in arranging a convention in 1868 excluding from consideration all claims for indirect damages, but this arrangement was unfavorably reported from the Committee on Foreign Affairs in the Senate. It was then that Charles Sumner, Chairman of the Committee, gave utterance to his astounding demands upon Great Britain. The direct claims of the United States, he contended, were no adequate compensation for its losses; the indirect claims must also be made good, particularly those based on the loss of the American merchant marine by transfer to the British flag. The direct or "individual" American losses amounted to $15,000,000. "But this leaves without recognition the vaster damage to commerce driven from the ocean, and that other damage, immense and infinite, caused by the prolongation of the war, all of which may be called *national* in contradistinction to *individual*." Losses to commerce he reckoned at $110,000,000, adding that this amount must be considered only an item in the bill, for the prolongation of the war was directly traceable to England. "The rebellion was suppressed at a cost of more than four thousand million dollars . . . through British intervention the war was doubled in duration; . . . England is justly responsible for the additional expenditure." Sumner's total bill against Great Britain, then, amounted to over $2,000,000,000; "everyone," said he, "can make the calculation."

Had an irresponsible member of Congress made these demands, they might have been dismissed as another effort to twist the British lion's tail; but Charles Sumner took himself seriously, expected others to take him seriously, and unhappily was taken seriously by a great number of his fellow countrymen. The explanation of his preposterous demand appeared subsequently in a memorandum which he prepared. To avoid all possible future clashes with Great Britain, he would have her withdraw from the American continents and the Western Hemisphere. Great Britain might discharge her financial obligations by transferring to the United States the whole of British America! And Sumner seems actually to have believed that he was promoting the cause of international good will by this tactless proposal.

For a time it was believed that Sumner spoke for the Administration, and public opinion in the United States was disposed to look upon his speech as a fair statement of American grievances and a just demand for compensation. The British Government, too, in view of the action of the Senate and the indiscreet utterances of the new American Minister in London, John Lothrop Motley, believed that President Grant favored an aggressive policy. Further negotiations were dropped. Both Governments, nevertheless, were desirous of coming to an understanding, though neither wished to take the first step.

Fortunately it happened that Caleb Cushing for the United States and John Rose for Canada were then engaged at Washington in the discussion of some matters affecting the two countries. In the course of informal conversations these accomplished diplomats planned for a *rapprochement*. Rose presented a memorandum suggesting that all questions in dispute be made the subject of a general negotiation and treaty. It was at this moment that Sumner came forward with his plan of compensation and obviously he stood in the way of any settlement. President Grant, however, already incensed by Motley's conduct and by Sumner's opposition to his own favorite project, the annexation of Santo Domingo, now broke definitely with both by removing Motley and securing Sumner's deposition from the chairmanship of the Committee on Foreign Affairs. The way was now prepared for an agreement with Great Britain.

On February 27, 1871, a Joint High Commission, composed of five distinguished representatives from each Government, began its memorable session at Washington. The outcome was the Treaty of Washington, signed on May 8, 1871. The most important question — the "Alabama Claims" — was by this agreement to be submitted to a tribunal of five arbitrators, one to be selected by the President of the United States, another by the Queen of

Great Britain, a third by the King of Italy, a fourth by the President of the Swiss Republic, and a fifth by the Emperor of Brazil. This tribunal was to meet at Geneva and was to base its award on three rules for the conduct of neutral nations: "First, to use due diligence to prevent the fitting out, . . . within its jurisdiction. of any vessel which it has reasonable ground to believe is intended to cruise . . . against a Power with which it is at peace . . . ; secondly, not to permit . . . either belligerent to make use of its ports or waters as a base of naval operations . . . ; thirdly, to exercise due diligence in its own ports and waters . . . to prevent any violation of the foregoing obligations and duties."

Another but less elaborate tribunal was to decide all other claims which had arisen out of the Civil War. Still another arbitration commission was to assess the amount which the United States was to pay by way of compensation for certain privileges connected with the fisheries. The vexed question of the possession of the San Juan Islands was to be left to the decision of the Emperor of Germany. A series of articles provided for the amicable settlement of border questions between the United States and Canada. Never before in history had such important controversies been submitted voluntarily to arbitration and judicial settlement.

The tribunal which met at Geneva in December was a body of distinguished men who proved fully equal to the gravity of their task. Charles Francis Adams was appointed to represent the United States; Sir Alexander Cockburn, to represent Great Britain; the commissioners from neutral States were also men of distinction. J. C. Bancroft Davis was agent for the United States, and William M. Evarts, Caleb Cushing, and Morrison R. Waite acted as counsel. The case for the United States was not presented in a manner worthy of the occasion. According to Adams the American contentions "were advanced with an aggressiveness of tone and attorney-like smartness, more appropriate to the wranglings of a quarter-sessions court than to pleadings before a grave international tribunal." The American counsel were instructed to insist not, indeed, on indemnity for the cost of two years of war, but on compensation because of the transfer of our commerce to the British merchant marine, by virtue of the clause of the treaty which read "acts committed by the several vessels which have given rise to the claims generally known as the 'Alabama Claims.'" British public opinion considered this contention an act of bad faith. Excitement in England rose to a high pitch and the Gladstone Ministry proposed to withdraw from the arbitration.

That the tribunal of arbitration did not end in utter failure was due to the wisdom and courage of Adams. At his suggestion the five arbitrators announced on June 19, 1872, that they would not consider claims for indirect damages, because such claims did "not constitute, upon the principles of international law applicable to such cases, good foundation for an award of compensation, or computations of damages between nations." These claims dismissed, the arbitrators entered into an examination of the direct American claims and on September 14, 1872, decided upon an award of fifteen and a half million dollars to the United States. The Treaty of Washington and the Geneva Tribunal constituted the longest step thus far taken by any two nations toward the settlement of their disputes by judicial process.

# CHAPTER III

## ALASKA AND ITS PROBLEMS

THE impulse for expansion upon which Buchanan floated his political raft into the presidency was not a party affair. It was felt by men of all party creeds, and it seemed for a moment to be the dominant national ideal. Slaveholders and other men who had special interests sought to make use of it, but the fundamental feeling did not rest on their support. American democracy, now confident of its growing strength, believed that the happiness of the people and the success of the institutions of the United States would prove a loadstone which would bring under the flag all peoples of the New World, while those of the Old World would strike off their shackles and remold their governments on the American pattern. Attraction, not compulsion, was the method to be used, and none of the pæans of American prophets in the editorials

or the fervid orations of the fifties proposed an
additional battleship or regiment.

No one saw this bright vision more clearly than
did William H. Seward, who became Secretary of
State under Lincoln.  Slight of build, pleasant, and
talkative, he gave an impression of intellectual distinction, based upon fertility rather than consistency of mind.  He was a disciple of John Quincy
Adams, but his tireless energy had in it too much
of nervous unrest to allow him to stick to his books
as did his master, and there was too wide a gap
between his beliefs and his practice.  He held as
idealistic views as any man of his generation, but he
believed so firmly that the right would win that he
disliked hastening its victory at the expense of bad
feeling.  He was shrewd, practical — maliciously
practical, many thought.  When, in the heat of
one of his perorations, a flash of his hidden fires
would arouse the distrust of the conservative, he
would appear to retract and try to smother the
flames in a cloud of conciliatory smoke.  Only the
restraining hand of Lincoln prevented him from
committing fatal blunders at the outset of the Civil
War, yet his handling of the threatening episode of
the French in Mexico showed a wisdom, a patient
tact, and a subtle ingenuity which make his conduct

of the affair a classic illustration of diplomacy at
almost its best.[1]

In 1861 Seward said that he saw Russia and
Great Britain building on the Arctic Ocean out-
posts on territory which should belong to his own
country, and that he expected the capital of the
great federal republic of the future would be in
the valley of Mexico. Yet he nevertheless retained
the sentiment he had expressed in 1846: "I would
not give one human life for all the continent that
remains to be annexed." The Civil War prevented for four years any action regarding expansion, and the same conspiracy which resulted in
the assassination of Lincoln brought Seward to
the verge of the grave. He recovered rapidly, however, and while on a recuperating trip through the
West Indies he worked for the peaceable annexation of the Danish Islands and Santo Domingo.
His friend, Charles Sumner, the chairman of the
Senate Committee on Foreign Affairs, was fram-
ing his remarkable project for the annexation of
Canada. President Johnson and, later, President
Grant endorsed parts of these plans. Denmark
and Santo Domingo were willing to acquiesce for

[1] See *Abraham Lincoln and the Union* and *The Hispanic Nations of
the New World* (in *The Chronicles of America*).

money, and Sumner believed, although he was preposterously wrong, that the incorporation of Canada in our Union would be welcomed by the best sentiment of England and of Canada.

To willing ears, therefore, came in 1867 the offer of the Russian Minister, Baron Stoeckl, to sell Alaska. The proposal did not raise a question which had been entirely unthought of. Even before the Civil War, numbers of people on the Pacific coast, far from being overawed by the responsibility of developing the immense territories which they already possessed, had petitioned the Government to obtain Alaska, and even the proper purchase price had been discussed. The reasons for Russia's decision to sell, however, have not been sufficiently investigated. It is apparent from the conduct of the negotiation that it was not a casual proposal but one in which Baron Stoeckl, at least, was deeply interested. It is to be remembered that at this time Russia's ambitions were in Asia, and that her chief rival was Great Britain. Russia's power was on land; the seas she could not hope to control. The first moment of war would put Russian rule in Alaska at the mercy of the British fleet. In those days when a Siberian railroad was an idle dream, this icebound region in America was so

remote from the center of Russian power that it
could be neither enjoyed nor protected. As Napoleon in 1803 preferred to see Louisiana in the
hands of the United States rather than in those of
his rival England, so Russia preferred Alaska to
fall to the United States rather than to Canada,
especially as she could by peaceful cession obtain
money into the bargain.

Seward was delighted with the opportunity, but
diplomatically concealed his satisfaction and bar-
gained closely. Stoeckl asked ten million dollars;
Seward offered five. Stoeckl proposed to split the
difference; Seward agreed, if Stoeckl would knock
off the odd half million. Stoeckl accepted, on condition that Seward add two hundred thousand as
special compensation to the Russian American Company. It was midnight of the 29th of March when
$7,200,000 was made the price. Seward roused
Sumner from bed, and the three worked upon the
form of a treaty until four o'clock in the morning.
No captains of industry could show greater decision.

The treaty, however, was not yet a fact. The
Senate must approve, and its approval could not
be taken for granted. The temper of the majority
of Americans toward expansion had changed. The
experiences of the later fifties had caused many to

look upon expansion as a Southern heresy. Carl Schurz a little later argued that we had already taken in all those regions the climate of which would allow healthy self-government and that we should annex no tropics. Hamilton Fish, then Secretary of State, wrote in 1873 that popular sentiment was, for the time being, against all expansion. In fact, among the people of the United States the idea was developing that expansion was contrary to their national policy, and their indisposition to expand became almost a passion. They rejected Santo Domingo and the Danish Islands and would not press any negotiations for Canada.

What saved the Alaska Treaty from a similar disapproval was not any conviction that Alaska was worth seven million dollars, although Sumner convinced those who took the trouble to read, that the financial bargain was not a bad one. The chief factor in the purchase of Alaska was almost pure sentiment. Throughout American history there has been a powerful tradition of friendliness between Russia and the United States, yet surely no two political systems have been in the past more diametrically opposed. The chief ground for friendship has doubtless been the great intervening distance which has reduced intercourse to a minimum.

Some slight basis for congeniality existed in the fact that the interests of both countries favored a similar policy of freedom upon the high seas. What chiefly influenced the public mind, however, was the attitude which Russia had taken during the Civil War. When the Grand Duke Alexis visited the United States in 1871, Oliver Wendell Holmes greeted him with the lines:

Bleak are our coasts with the blasts of December,
Thrilling and warm are the hearts that remember
Who was our friend when the world was our foe.

This Russian friendship had presented itself dramatically to the public at a time when American relations with Great Britain were strained, for Russian fleets had in 1863 suddenly appeared in the harbors of New York and San Francisco. These visits were actually made with a sole regard for Russian interests and in anticipation of the outbreak of a general European war, which the Czar then feared. The appearance of the fleets, however, was for many years popularly supposed to signify sympathy with the Union and a willingness to defend it from attack by Great Britain and France. Many conceived the ingenuous idea that the purchase price of Alaska was really the American half of a secret bargain of which the fleets were the Russian part. Public opinion, therefore, regarded the purchase of Alaska in the light of a favor to Russia and demanded that the favor be granted.

Thus of all the schemes of expansion in the fifty years between the Mexican and the Spanish wars, for the Gadsden Purchase of 1853 was really only a rectification of boundary, this alone came to fruition. Seward could well congratulate himself on his alertness in seizing an opportunity and on his management of the delicate political aspects of the purchase. Without his promptness the golden opportunity might have passed and never recurred. Yet he could never have saved this fragment of his policy had not the American people cherished for Russia a sentimental friendship which was intensified at the moment by anger at the supposed sympathy of Great Britain for the South. If Russia hoped by ceding Alaska to involve the United States in difficulties with her rival Great Britain, her desire was on one occasion nearly gratified. The only profit which the United States derived from this new possession was for many years drawn from the seal fishery. The same generation of Americans which allowed the extermination of the buffalo for lap robes found in the

sealskin sack the hall mark of wealth and fashion.
While, however, the killing of the buffalo was allowed to go on without official check, the Government in 1870 inaugurated a system to preserve the
seal herds which was perhaps the earliest step in
a national conservation policy.  The sole right of
killing was given to the Alaska Commercial Company with restrictions under which it was believed that the herds would remain undiminished.
The catch was limited to one hundred thousand
a year; it was to include only male seals; and it
was to be limited to the breeding grounds on the
Pribilof Islands.

The seals, however, did not confine themselves
to American territory.  During the breeding season
they ranged far and wide within a hundred miles of
their islands; and during a great part of the year
they were to be found far out in the Pacific.  The
value of their skins attracted the adventurous of
many lands, but particularly Canadians; and Van-
couver became the greatest center for deep-sea
sealing.  The Americans saw the development of
the industry with anger and alarm.  Considering
the seals as their own, they naturally resented this
unlimited exploitation by outsiders when Americans themselves were so strictly limited by law.

They also believed that the steady diminution of the herds was due to the reckless methods of their rivals, particularly the use of explosives which destroyed many animals to secure a few perfect skins.

Public opinion on the Pacific coast sought a remedy and soon found one in the terms of the treaty of purchase. That document, in dividing Alaska from Siberia, described a line of division running through Bering Sea, and in 1881 the Acting Secretary of the Treasury propounded the theory that this line divided not merely the islands but the water as well. There was a widespread feeling that all Bering Sea within this line was American territory and that all intruders from other nations were poachers. In accordance with this theory, the revenue cutter *Corwin* in 1886 seized three British vessels and haled their skippers before the United States District Court of Sitka. Thomas F. Bayard, then Secretary of State under President Cleveland, did not recognize this theory of interpreting the treaty, but endeavored to right the grievance by a joint agreement with France, Germany, Japan, Russia, and Great Britain, the sealing nations, "for the better protection of the fur seal fisheries in Bering Sea."

A solution had been almost reached, when Canada

interposed. Lord Morley has remarked, in his *Recollections*, how the voice of Canada fetters Great Britain in her negotiations with the United States. While Bayard was negotiating an agreement concerning Bering Sea which was on the whole to the advantage of the United States, he completed a similar convention on the more complicated question of the northeastern or Atlantic fisheries which was more important to Canada. This latter convention was unfavorably reported by the Senate Committee on Foreign Affairs, which foreshadowed rejection. Thereupon, in May, 1888, Lord Salisbury, the British Foreign Minister, withdrew from the Bering Sea negotiation.

At this critical moment Cleveland gave place to Harrison, and Bayard was succeeded by James G. Blaine, the most interesting figure in our diplomatic activities of the eighties. These years marked the lowest point in the whole history of our relations with other countries, both in the character of our agents and in the nature of the public opinion to which they appealed. Blaine was undoubtedly the most ill-informed of our great diplomats; yet a trace of greatness lingers about him. The exact reverse of John Quincy Adams, he knew neither law nor history, and he did not always inspire others with confidence in his integrity. On the other hand, the magnetic charm of his personality won many to a devotion such as none of our great men except Clay has received. Blaine saw, moreover, though through a glass darkly, farther along the path which the United States was to take than did any of his contemporaries. It was his fate to deal chiefly in controversy with those accomplished diplomats, Lord Salisbury and Lord Granville, and it must have been among the relaxations of their office to point out tactfully the defects and errors in his dispatches. Nevertheless when he did not misread history or misquote precedents but wielded the broadsword of equity, he often caught the public conscience, and then he was not an opponent to be despised.

Blaine at once undertook the defense of the contention that Bering Sea was "closed" and the exclusive property of the United States, in spite of the fact that this position was opposed to the whole trend of American opinion, which from the days of the Revolution had always stood for freedom of the high seas and the limitation of the water rights of particular nations to the narrowest limits. The United States and Great Britain had jointly protested against the Czar's ukase of 1821, which had asserted Russia's claim to Bering Sea as territorial waters; and if Russia had not possessed it in 1821, we certainly could not have bought it in 1867. In the face of Canadian opinion, Great Britain could never consent, even for the sake of peace, to a position as unsound as it was disadvantageous to Canadian industry. Nor did Blaine's contention that the seals were domestic animals belonging to us, and therefore subject to our protection while wandering through the ocean, carry conviction to lawyers familiar with the fascinating intricacies of the law, domestic and international, relating to migratory birds and beasts. To the present generation it seems amusing that Blaine defended his basic contention quite as much on the ground of the inhumanity of destroying the seals as of its economic wastefulness. Yet Blaine rallied Congress to his support, as well as a great part of American sentiment.

The situation, which had now become acute, was aggravated by the fact that most American public men of this period did not separate their foreign and domestic politics. Too many sought to secure the important Irish vote by twisting the tail of the British lion. The Republicans, in particular, sought to identify protection with patriotism and were making much of the fact that the recall of Lord Sackville-West, the British Minister, had been forced because he had advised a correspondent to vote for Cleveland. It spoke volumes for the fundamental good sense of the two nations that, when relations were so strained, they could agree to submit their differences to arbitration. For this happy outcome credit must be given to the cooler heads on both sides, but equal credit must be given to their legacy from the cool heads which had preceded them. The United States and Great Britain had acquired the habit of submitting to judicial decision their disputes, even those closely touching honor, and this habit kept them steady.

In accepting arbitration in 1892, the United States practically gave up her case, although Blaine undoubtedly believed it could be defended, and in spite of the fact that it was ably presented by John W. Foster from a brief prepared by the American counsel, Edward J. Phelps, Frederic R. Coudert, and James C. Carter | The tribunal assembled at Paris decided that Bering Sea was open and determined certain facts upon which a subsequent commission assessed damages of nearly half a million against the United States for the seizure of British vessels during the period in which the American claim was being asserted. Blaine, however, did not lose everything. The treaty contained the extraordinary provision that the arbitration tribunal, in case it decided against the United States, was to draw up regulations for the protection of the seal herds. These regulations when drafted did not prove entirely satisfactory, and bound only the United States and Great Britain. It required many years and much tinkering to bring about the reasonably satisfactory arrangement that is now in force. Yet to leave to an international tribunal not merely the decision of a disputed case but the legislation necessary to regulate an international property was in itself a great step in the development of world polity. The charlatan who almost brought on war by maintaining an indefensible case was also the statesman who made perhaps the greatest single advance in the conservation of the world's resources by international regulation.

# CHAPTER IV

## BLAINE AND PAN-AMERICANISM

DURING the half century that intervened between John Quincy Adams and James G. Blaine, the Monroe Doctrine, it was commonly believed, had prevented the expansion of the territories of European powers in the Americas. It had also relieved the United States both of the necessity of continual preparation for war and of that constant tension in which the perpetual shifting of the European balance of power held the nations of that continent. But the Monroe Doctrine was not solely responsible for these results. Had it not been for the British Navy, the United States would in vain have proclaimed its disapproval of encroachment. Nor, had Europe continued united, could the United States have withstood European influence; but Canning's policy had practically destroyed Metternich's dream of unity maintained by intervention, and in 1848 that whole structure went hopelessly tumbling before a new order. Yet British policy, too, failed of full realization, for British statesmen always dreamed of an even balance in continental Europe which Great Britain could incline to her wishes, whereas it usually proved necessary, in order to preserve a balance at all, for her to join one side or the other. Divided Europe therefore stood opposite united America, and our inferior strength was enhanced by an advantageous position.

The insecurity of the American position was revealed during the Civil War. When the United States divided within, the strength of the nation vanished. The hitherto suppressed desires of European nations at once manifested themselves. Spain, never satisfied that her American empire was really lost, at once leaped to take advantage of the change. On a trumped up invitation of some of the inhabitants of Santo Domingo, she invaded the formerly Spanish portion of the island and she began war with Peru in the hope of acquiring at least some of the Pacific islands belonging to that state.

More formidable were the plans of Napoleon III, for the French, too, remembered the glowing promise of their earlier American dominions. They had not forgotten that the inhabitants of the Americas as far north as the southern borders of the United

States were of Latin blood, at least so far as they were of European origin. In Montevideo there was a French colony, and during the forties France had been active in proffering her advice in South American disputes. When the second French Republic had been proclaimed in 1848, one of the French ministers in South America saw a golden chance for his country to assume the leadership of all Latin America, which was at that time suspicious of the designs of the United States and alarmed by its rapid expansion at the expense of Mexico. With the power of the American Government neutralized in 1861, and with the British Navy immobilized by the necessity of French friendship, which the "Balance" made just then of paramount interest to Great Britain, Napoleon III determined to establish in Mexico an empire under French influence.

It is instructive to notice that General Bernhardi states, in *Germany and the Next War* which has attracted such wide attention and which has done so much to convince Americans of the bad morals of autocracy, that Great Britain lost her great chance of world dominance by not taking active advantage of this situation, as did France and Spain. It is indeed difficult to see what would have been the outcome had Great Britain also played at that time an aggressive and selfish part. She stayed her hand, but many British statesmen were keenly interested in the struggle, from the point of view of British interests. They did not desire territory, but they foresaw that the permanent separation of the two parts of the United States would leave the country shorn of weight in the affairs of the Western Hemisphere. North and South, if separated, would each inevitably seek European support, and the isolation of the United States and its claim to priority in American affairs would disappear. The balance of power would extend itself to the Western Hemisphere and the assumption of a sphere of influence would vanish with the unity of the United States.

Nor did the close of the Civil War reveal less clearly than its beginning the real international position of the United States. When the country once more acquired unity, these European encroachments were renounced, and dreams of colonial empire in America vanished. There was a moment's questioning as to the reality of the triumph of the North — a doubt that the South might rise if foreign war broke out; but the uncertainty was soon dispelled. It was somewhat embarrassing, if not humiliating, for the Emperor of the French to withdraw from his Mexican undertaking, but the way was smoothed for him by the finesse of Seward. By 1866 the international position of the United States was reëstablished and was perhaps the stronger for having been tested.

In all these years, however, the positive side of the Monroe Doctrine, the development of friendly coöperation between the nations of America under the leadership of the United States, had made no progress. In fact, with the virtual disappearance of the American merchant marine after the Civil War, the influence of the United States diminished. Great Britain with her ships, her trade, and her capital, at that time actually counted for much more, while German trade expanded rapidly in the seventies and eighties and German immigration into Brazil gave Prussia a lever hold, the ultimate significance of which is not even yet fully evident.

Under these circumstances, Blaine planned to play a brilliant rôle as Secretary of State in President Garfield's Cabinet. Though the President was his personal friend, Blaine regarded him as his inferior in practical statecraft and planned to make his own foreign policy the notable feature of the Administration. His hopes were dashed, however, by the assassination of Garfield and by the accession of President Arthur. The new Secretary of State, F. T. Frelinghuysen, reversed nearly all of his predecessor's policies. When Blaine returned to the Department of State in 1889, he found a less sympathetic chief in President Harrison and a less brilliant rôle to play. Whether his final retirement before the close of the Harrison Administration was due directly to the conflict of views which certainly existed or was a play on his part for the presidency and for complete control is a question that has never been completely settled.

Narrow as was Blaine's view of world affairs, impossible as was his conception of an America divided from Europe economically and spiritually as well as politically and of an America united in itself by a provoked and constantly irritated hostility to Europe, he had an American program which, taken by itself, was definite, well conceived, and in a sense prophetic. It is interesting to note that in referring to much the same relationship, Blaine characteristically spoke of the United States as "Elder Sister" of the South American republics, while Theodore Roosevelt, at a later period, conceived the rôle to be that of a policeman wielding the "Big Stick."

Blaine's first aim was to establish peace in the

Western Hemisphere by offering American mediation in the disputes of sister countries. When
he first took office in 1881, the prolonged and
bitter war existing between Chili, Bolivia, and Peru
for the control of the nitrate fields which lay just
where the territories of the three abutted, provided a convenient opportunity. If he could restore peace on an equitable basis here, he would do
much to establish the prestige of the United States
as a wise and disinterested counselor in Spanish
American affairs. In this his first diplomatic undertaking, there appeared, however, one of the
weaknesses of execution which constantly interfered with the success of his plans. He did not
know how to sacrifice politics to statesmanship,
and he appointed as his agents men so incompe-
tent that they aggravated rather than settled the
difficulty. Later he saw his mistake and made
a new and admirable appointment in the case
of Mr. William H. Trescot of South Carolina.
Blaine himself, however, lost office before new
results could be obtained; and Frelinghuysen
recalled Trescot and abandoned the attempt to
force peace.

A second object of Blaine's policy was to prevent
disputes between Latin American and European

powers from becoming dangerous by acting as mediator between them.    When he took office, France
was endeavoring to collect from Venezuela a claim
which was probably just.    When Venezuela proved
obdurate, France proposed to seize her custom
houses and to collect the duties until the debt was
paid.    Blaine protested, urged Venezuela to pay,
and suggested that the money be sent through
the American agent at Caracas.    He further proposed that, should Venezuela not pay within three
months, the United States should seize the custom
houses, collect the money, and pay it to France.
Again his short term prevented him from carrying
out his policy, but it is nevertheless of interest as
anticipating the plan actually followed by President
Roosevelt in the case of Santo Domingo.

Blaine was just as much opposed to the peaceful
penetration of European influence in the Western
Hemisphere as to its forceful expression.    The project of a canal across the Isthmus of Panama, to be
built and owned by a French company, had already
aroused President Hayes on March 8, 1880, to remark: "The policy of this country is a canal under American control.    The United States cannot
consent to the surrender of this control to any European power or to any combination of European

powers." Blaine added that the passage of hostile troops through such a canal when either the United States or Colombia was at war, as the terms of guarantee of the new canal allowed, was "no more admissible than on the railroad lines joining the Atlantic and Pacific shores of the United States."

It is characteristic of Blaine that, when he wrote this dispatch, he was apparently in complete ignorance of the existence of the Clayton-Bulwer Treaty, in which the United States accepted the exactly opposite principles — had agreed to a canal under a joint international guarantee and open to the use of all in time of war as well as of peace. Discovering this obstacle, he set to work to demolish it by announcing to Great Britain that the treaty was antiquated, thirty years old, that the development of the American Pacific slope had changed conditions, and that, should the treaty be observed and such a canal remain unfortified, the superiority of the British fleet would give the nation complete control. Great Britain, however, could scarcely be expected to regard a treaty as defunct from old age at thirty years, especially as she also possessed a developing Pacific coast. Moreover, if the treaty was to British advantage, at least the United States had accepted it. Great Britain, therefore refused to admit that the treaty was not in full force. Blaine then urged the building of an American canal across the Isthmus of Nicaragua, in defiance of the Clayton-Bulwer Treaty — a plan which received the support of even President Arthur, under whom a treaty for the purpose was negotiated with the Republic of Nicaragua. Before this treaty was ratified by the Senate, however, Grover Cleveland, who had just become President, withdrew it. He believed in the older policy, and refused his sanction to the new treaty on the ground that such a canal "must be for the world's benefit, a trust for mankind, to be removed from the chance of domination by any single power."

The crowning glory of Blaine's system, as he planned it, was the coöperation of the American republics for common purposes. He did not share Seward's dream that they would become incorporated States of the Union, but he went back to Henry Clay and the Panama Congress of 1826 for his ideal. During his first term of office he invited the republics to send representatives to Washington to discuss arbitration, but his successor in office feared that such a meeting of "a partial group of our friends" might offend Europe, which indeed was not improbably part of Blaine's intention. On resuming office, Blaine finally arranged the meeting of a Pan-American Congress in the United States. Chosen to preside, he presented an elaborate program, including a plan for arbitrating disputes; commercial reciprocity; the establishment of uniform weights and measures, of international copyright, trade-marks and patents, and of common coinage; improvement of communications; and other subjects. At the same time he exerted himself to secure in the McKinley Tariff Bill, which was just then under consideration, a provision for reciprocity of trade with American countries. This meeting was not a complete success, since Congress gave him only half of what he wanted by providing for reciprocity but making it general instead of purely American. Nevertheless one permanent and solid result was secured in the establishment of the Bureau of American Republics at Washington, which has become a clearing house of ideas and a visible bond of common interests and good feeling.

Throughout the years of Blaine's prominence, the public took more interest in his bellicose encounters with Europe, and particularly with Great Britain, than in his constructive American policy; and he failed to secure for either an assured popular

support.  His attempt to widen the gulf between
Europe and America was indeed absurd at a time
when the cable, the railroad, and the steamship
were rendering the world daily smaller and more
closely knit, and when the spirit of democracy,
rapidly permeating western Europe, was breaking
down the distinction in political institutions which
had given point to the pronouncement of 1823.
Nevertheless Blaine did actually feel the changing
industrial conditions at home which were destroying American separateness, and he made a genuine
attempt to find a place for the United States in the
world, without the necessity of sharing the responsibilities of all the world, by making real that interest in its immediate neighbors which his country
had announced in 1823.  Even while Blaine was
working on his plan of "America for the Americans," events were shaping the most important
extension of the interests of the United States
which had taken place since 1823.

5

# CHAPTER V

## THE UNITED STATES AND THE PACIFIC

Long before the westward march of Americans had brought their flag to the Pacific, that ocean was familiar to their mariners. From Cape Horn to Canton and the ports of India, there ploughed the stately merchantmen of Salem, Providence, and Newburyport, exchanging furs and ginseng for teas, silks, the "Canton blue" which is today so cherished a link with the past, and for the lacquer cabinets and carved ivory which give distinction to many a New England home. Meanwhile the sturdy whalers of New Bedford scoured the whole ocean for sperm oil and whalebone, and the incidents of their self-reliant three-year cruises acquainted them with nearly every coral and volcanic isle. Early in the century missionaries also began to brave the languor of these oases of leisure and the appetite of their cannibalistic inhabitants.

The interest of the Government was bound to

follow its adventurous citizens. In 1820 the United States appointed a consular agent at Honolulu; in the thirties and forties it entered into treaty relations with Siam, Borneo, and China; and owing to circumstances which were by no means accidental it had the honor of persuading Japan to open her ports to the world. As early as 1797 an American vessel chartered by the Dutch had visited Nagasaki. From time to time American sailors had been shipwrecked on the shores of Japan, and the United States had more than once picked up and sought to return Japanese castaways. In 1846 an official expedition under Commodore Biddle was sent to establish relationships with Japan but was unsuccessful. In 1853 Commodore Perry bore a message from the President to the Mikado which demanded — though the demand was couched in courteous language — "friendship, commerce, a supply of coal and provisions, and protection for our shipwrecked people." After a long hesitation the Mikado yielded. Commodore Perry's success was due not solely to the care with which his expedition was equipped for its purpose nor to his diplomatic skill but in part to the fact that other countries were known to be on the very point of forcing an entrance into the seclusion of Japan. Few Americans realize how close, indeed, were the relations established with Japan by the United States. The treaty which Townsend Harris negotiated in 1858 stated that "The President of the United States, at the request of the Japanese Government, will act as a friendly mediator in such matters of difference as may arise between the Government of Japan and any European power." Through his personal efforts Harris may almost be said to have become the chief adviser of the Japanese Government in the perplexities which it encountered on entering international society.

Not only did the United States allow itself a closer intimacy with this new Pacific power than it would have done with a state of Europe, but it exhibited a greater freedom in dealing with the European powers themselves in the Far East than at home or in America. In 1863 the United States joined — in fact, in the absence of a naval force it strained a point by chartering a vessel for the purpose — with a concert of powers to force the opening of the Shimonoseki Straits; subsequently acting with Great Britain, France, and the Netherlands, the United States secured an indemnity to pay the cost of the expedition; and in 1866 it united with the same powers to secure a convention by which Japan bound herself to establish certain tariff regulations.

Nor were the relations of the United States with the Pacific Ocean and its shores confined to trade and international obligations. The American flag waved over more than ships and a portion of the Pacific coast. Naval officers more than once raised it over islands which they christened, and Congress authorized the President to exercise temporary authority over islands from which American citizens were removing guano and to prevent foreign encroachment while they were so engaged. In the eighties, fifty such islands of the Pacific were in the possession of the United States.

In 1872 an American naval officer made an agreement with the local chieftain of Tutuila, one of the Samoan Islands, for the use of Pago Pago, which was the best harbor in that part of the ocean. The United States drifted into more intimate relationship with the natives until in 1878 it made a treaty with the Samoan king allowing Americans to use Pago Pago as a coaling station. In return the United States agreed: "If unhappily, any differences should have arisen, or shall hereafter arise, between the Samoan government and any other government in amity with the United States, the government of the latter will employ its good offices for the purpose of adjusting those differences upon a satisfactory and solid foundation." In 1884 the Senate insisted on securing a similar harbor concession from Hawaii, and within the next few years the American Navy began to arise again from its ashes. The obligation incurred in exchange for this concession, however, although it resembled that in the Japanese treaty, was probably an unreflecting act of good nature for, if it meant anything, it was an entangling engagement such as the vast majority of Americans were still determined to avoid.

The natives of Samoa did not indulge in cannibalism but devoted the small energy the climate gave them to the social graces and to pleasant wars. They were governed by local kings and were loosely united under a chief king. At Apia, the capital, were three hundred foreigners, nearly all connected in one way or another with trade. This commerce had long been in the hands of English and Americans, but now the aggressive Germans were rapidly winning it away. Three consuls, representing the United States, Great Britain, and Germany, spent their time in exaggerating their functions and in circumventing the plots of which they suspected each other. The stage was set for comic opera, the treaty with the United States was part of the plot, and several acts had already been played, when Bismarck suddenly injected a tragic element.

In 1884, at the time when the German statesman began to see the vision of a Teutonic world empire and went about seeking places in the sun, the German consul in Samoa, by agreement with King Malietoa, raised the German flag over the royal hut, with a significance which was all too obvious. In 1886 the American consul countered this move by proclaiming a United States protectorate. The German consul then first pressed home a quarrel with the native king at a time opportunely coinciding with the arrival of a German warship, the *Adler;* he subsequently deposed him and put up Tamasese in his stead. The apparently more legitimate successor, Mataafa, roused most of the population under his leadership. The *Adler* steamed about the islands shelling Mataafa villages, and the American consul steamed after him, putting his launch between the *Adler* and the shore. In the course of these events, on December 18, 1888, Mataafa ambushed a German landing party and killed fifty of its members.

German public opinion thereupon vociferously demanded a punishment which would establish the place of Germany as a colonial power in the Pacific.

Great Britain, however, was not disposed to give her growing rival a free hand. The United States was appealed to under the Treaty of 1878, and American sentiment determined to protect the Samoans in their heroic fight for self-government. All three nations involved sent warships to Apia, and through the early spring of 1889 their chancelleries and the press were prepared to hear momentarily that some one's temper had given way in the tropic heat and that blood had been shed — with what consequences on the other side of the globe no man could tell.

Very different, however, was the news that finally limped in, for there was no cable. On March 16, 1889, a hurricane had swept the islands, wrecking all but one of the warships. The common distress had brought about coöperation among all parties. Tales of mutual help and mutual praise of natives and the three nations filled the dispatches. The play turned out to be a comedy after all. Yet difficulties remained which could be met only by joint action. A commission of the three nations therefore was arranged to meet in Berlin. The United States insisted on native government; Germany, on foreign control. Finally they agreed to a compromise in the form of a General Act, to which Samoa consented. The native government was retained, but the control was given to a Chief Justice and a President of the Municipal Council of Apia, who were to be foreigners chosen by the three powers. Their relative authority is indicated by the fact that the king was to receive $1800 a year, the Chief Justice, $6000, and the President, $5000.

Small as was the immediate stake, this little episode was remarkably significant of the trend of American development. Begun under Grant and concluded under Blaine and Harrison, the policy of the United States was the creation of no one mind or party nor did it accord with American traditions. Encountering European powers in the Pacific, with no apparent hesitation though without any general intent, the United States entered into coöperative agreements with them relating to the native governments which it would never have thought proper or possible in other parts of the world. The United States seemed to be evolving a new policy for the protection of its interests in the Pacific. This first clash with the rising colonial power of Germany has an added interest because it revealed a fundamental similarity in colonial policy between the United States and Great Britain, even though they were prone to quarrel when adjusting Anglo-American relations.

While the Samoan affair seemed an accidental happening, there was taking shape in the Pacific another episode which had a longer history and was more significant of the expansion of American interests in that ocean. Indeed, with the Pacific coast line of the United States, with the superb harbors of San Francisco, Portland, and Puget Sound, and with Alaska stretching its finger tips almost to Asia, even Blaine could not resist the lure of the East, though he endeavored to reconcile American traditions of isolation with oceanic expansion. Of all the Pacific archipelagoes, the Hawaiian Islands lie nearest to the shores of the United States. Although they had been discovered to the European world by the great English explorer, Captain Cook, their intercourse had, for geographic reasons, always been chiefly with the United States. Whalers continually resorted to them for supplies. Their natives shipped on American vessels and came in numbers to California in early gold-mining days. American missionaries attained their most striking success in the Hawaiian Islands and not only converted the majority of the natives but assisted the successive kings in their government. The descendants of these missionaries continued to live on the islands and became the nucleus of a white population which waxed rich and powerful by the abundant production of sugar cane on that volcanic soil.

In view of this tangible evidence of intimacy on the part of the United States with the Hawaiian Islands, Webster in 1842 brought them within the scope of the Monroe Doctrine by declaring that European powers must not interfere with their government.   Marcy, Secretary of State, framed a treaty of annexation in 1853, but the Hawaiian Government withdrew its assent.   Twenty years later Secretary Fish wrote: "There seems to be a strong desire on the part of many persons in the islands, representing large interests and great wealth, to become annexed to the United States and while there are, as I have already said, many and influential persons in the country who question the policy of any insular acquisition, perhaps even any extension of territorial limits, there are also those of influence and wise foresight who see a future that must extend the jurisdiction and the limits of this nation, and that will require a resting spot in the mid-ocean, between the Pacific coast and the vast domains of Asia, which are now opening to commerce and Christian civilization."

All immediate action, however, was confined to a specially intimate treaty of reciprocity which was signed in 1875, and which secured a substantial American domination in commerce. When Blaine became Secretary of State in 1881, he was, or at least he affected to be, seriously alarmed at the possibility of foreign influence in Hawaiian affairs, particularly on the part of Great Britain. The native population was declining, and should it continue to diminish, he believed that the United States must annex the islands. "Throughout the continent, north and south," he wrote, "wherever a foothold is found for American enterprise, it is quickly occupied, and the spirit of adventure, which seeks its outlet, in the mines of South America and the railroads of Mexico, would not be slow to avail itself of openings of assured and profitable enterprise even in mid-ocean." As the feeling grew in the United States that these islands really belonged to the American continent, Blaine even invited Hawaii to send representatives to the Pan-American Congress of 1889. When he again became Secretary of State, he was prepared to give indirect support at least to American interests, for the new queen, Liliuokalani, was supposed to be under British influence. On the arrival of a British gunboat in Honolulu, J. L. Stevens, the American Minister, went so far as to write on February 8, 1892: "At this time there seems to be no immediate prospect of its being safe to have the harbor of Honolulu left without an American vessel of war."

Revolution was, indeed, impending in Hawaii. On January 14, 1893, the Queen abolished the later constitution under which the Americans had exercised great power, and in its place she proclaimed the restoration of the old constitution which established an absolutism modified by native home rule. At two o'clock on the afternoon of the 16th of January, the resident Americans organized a committee of safety; at half-past four United States marines landed at the call of Stevens. The Queen was thereupon deposed, a provisional government was organized, and at its request Stevens assumed for the United States the "protection" of the islands. Without delay, John W. Foster, who had just succeeded Blaine as Secretary of State, drew up a treaty of annexation, which he immediately submitted to the Senate.

On March 4, 1893, Cleveland became President for the second time. He at once withdrew the treaty and appointed James H. Blount special commissioner to investigate the facts of the revolt. While the report of Commissioner Blount did not, indeed, convict Stevens of conspiring to bring about the uprising, it left the impression that the revolt would not have taken place and certainly could not have succeeded except for the presence of the United States marines and the support of the United States Minister. Cleveland recalled Stevens and the marines, and requested the provisional government to restore the Queen. This Sanford Ballard Dole, the President of the new republic, refused to do, on the contention that President Cleveland had no right to interfere in the domestic affairs of Hawaii. On the legality or propriety of Stevens's conduct, opinion in Congress was divided; but with regard to Dole's contention, both the Senate and the House were agreed that the islands should maintain their own domestic government without interference from the United States. Thus left to themselves, the Americans in Hawaii bided their time until public opinion in the United States should prove more favorable to annexation.

# CHAPTER VI

## VENEZUELA

PROBABLY no President ever received so much personal abuse in his own day as did Grover Cleveland. In time, however, his sterling integrity and fundamental courage, his firm grasp of the higher administrative duties of his office, won the approval of his countrymen, and a repentant public sentiment has possibly gone too far in the other direction of acclaiming his statesmanship. Unlike Blaine, Cleveland thought soundly and consistently; but he was more obstinate, his vision was often narrower, and he was notably lacking both in constructive power and in tact, particularly in foreign relations. In his first Administration, through his Secretary of State, Thomas F. Bayard, Cleveland had negotiated fairly amicably with Great Britain, and when he failed to secure the Senate's assent to a treaty on the irritating question of the northeastern fisheries, he arranged a *modus vivendi* which served for many years. In American affairs he opposed not only the annexation of Hawaii but also the development of the spirit of Pan-Americanism. He was, however, no more disposed than was Blaine to permit infractions of that negative side of the Monroe Doctrine which forbade European interference in America. His second Administration brought to the forefront of world diplomacy an issue involving this traditional principle.

The only European possession in South America at this time was Guiana, fronting on the Atlantic north of Brazil and divided among France, Holland, and Great Britain. Beyond British Guiana, the westernmost division, lay Venezuela. Between the two stretched a vast tract of unoccupied tropical jungle. Somewhere there must have been a boundary, but where, no man could tell. The extreme claim of Great Britain would have given her command of the mouth of the Orinoco, while that of Venezuela would practically have eliminated British Guiana. Efforts to settle this long-standing dispute were unavailing. Venezuela had from time to time suggested arbitration but wished to throw the whole area into court. Great Britain insisted upon reserving a minimum territory and would submit to judicial decision only the land west of what was known as the Schomburgk line of 1840. As early as 1876 Venezuela appealed to the United States, "the most powerful and oldest of the Republics of the new continent," for its "powerful moral support in disputes with European nations." Several times the United States proffered its good offices to Great Britain, but to no effect. The satisfactory settlement of the question grew more difficult as time went on, particularly after the discovery of gold in the disputed region had given a new impulse to occupation.

President Cleveland took a serious view of this controversy because it seemed to involve more than a boundary dispute. To his mind it called into question the portion of Monroe's message which, in 1823, stated that "the American continents . . . are henceforth not to be considered as subjects for future colonization by any European powers." According to this dictum, boundaries existed between all nations and colonies of America; the problem was merely to find these boundaries. If a European power refused to submit such a question to judicial decision, the inference must be made that it was seeking to extend its boundaries. In December, 1894, Cleveland expressed to Congress his hope that an arbitration would be arranged and instructed his

6

Secretary of State to present vigorously to Great Britain the view of the United States.

Richard Olney of Boston, a lawyer of exceptional ability and of the highest professional standing, was then Secretary of State. His Venezuela dispatch, however, was one of the most undiplomatic documents ever issued by the Department of State. He did not confine himself to a statement of his case, wherein any amount of vigor would have been permissible, but ran his unpracticed eye unnecessarily over the whole field of American diplomacy. "That distance and three thousand miles of intervening ocean make any permanent political union between a European and an American state unnatural and inexpedient," may have been a philosophic axiom to many in Great Britain as well as in the United States, but it surely did not need reiteration in this state paper, and Olney at once exposed himself to contradiction by adding the phrase, "will hardly be denied." Entirely ignoring the sensitive pride of the Spanish Americans and thinking only of Europe, he continued: "To-day the United States is practically sovereign on this continent, and its fiat is law upon the subjects to which it confines its interposition."

The President himself did not run into any such

uncalled-for extravagance of expression, but his statement of the American position did not thereby lose in vigor. When he had received the reply of the British Government refusing to recognize the interest of the United States in the case, Cleveland addressed himself, on December 17, 1895, to Congress. In stating the position of the Government of the United States, he declared that to determine the true boundary line was its right, duty, and interest. He recommended that the Government itself appoint a commission for this purpose, and he asserted that this line, when found, must be maintained as the lawful boundary. Should Great Britain continue to exercise jurisdiction beyond it, the United States must resist by every means in its power. "In making these recommendations I am fully alive to the responsibility incurred, and keenly realize all the consequences that may follow." Yet "there is no calamity which a great nation can invite which equals that which follows a supine submission to wrong and injustice and the consequent loss of national self-respect and honor beneath which are shielded and defended a people's safety and greatness."

Perhaps no American document relating to diplomacy ever before made so great a stir in the world. Its unexpectedness enhanced its effect, even in the United States, for the public had not been sufficiently aware of the shaping of this international episode to be psychologically prepared for the imminence of war. Unlike most Anglo-American diplomacy, this had been a long-range negotiation, with notes exchanged between the home offices instead of personal conferences. People blenched at the thought of war; stocks fell; the attention of the whole world was arrested. The innumerable and intimate bonds of friendship and interest which would thus have to be broken merely because of an insignificant jog in a boundary remote from both the nations made war between the United States and Great Britain seem absolutely inconceivable, until people realized that neither country could yield without an admission of defeat both galling to national pride and involving fundamental principles of conduct and policy for the future.

Great Britain in particular stood amazed at Cleveland's position. The general opinion was that peace must be maintained and that diplomats must find a formula which would save both peace and appearances. Yet before this public opinion could be diplomatically formulated, a new episode shook the British sense of security. Germany again appeared as a menace and, as in the case of Samoa, the international situation thus produced tended to develop a realization of the kinship between Great Britain and the United States. Early in January, 1896, the Jameson raid into the Transvaal was defeated, and the Kaiser immediately telegraphed his congratulations to President Krüger. In view of the possibilities involved in this South African situation, British public opinion demanded that her diplomats maintain peace with the United States, with or without the desired formula.

The British Government, however, was not inclined to act with undue haste. It became apparent even to the most panicky that war with the United States could not come immediately, for the American Commission of Inquiry must first report. For a time Lord Salisbury hoped that Congress would not support the President — a contingency which not infrequently happened under Cleveland's Administration. On this question of foreign relations, however, Congress stood squarely behind the President. Lord Salisbury then toyed with the hope that the matter might be delayed until Cleveland's term expired, in the hope he might have an opportunity of dealing with a less strenuous successor.

In the summer of 1896, John Hay, an intimate

friend of Major McKinley, the probable Republican candidate for the presidency, was in England, where he was a well-known figure. There he met privately Arthur J. Balfour, representing Lord Salisbury, and Sir William Harcourt, the leader of the Opposition. Hay convinced them that a change in the Administration of his country would involve no retreat from the existing American position. The British Government thereupon determined to yield but attempted to cover its retreat by merging the question with one of general arbitration. This proposal, however, was rejected, and Lord Salisbury then agreed to "an equitable settlement" of the Venezuela question by empowering the British Ambassador at Washington to begin negotiations "either with the representative of Venezuela or with the Government of the United States acting as the friend of Venezuela."

The achievement of the Administration consisted in forcing Great Britain to recognize the interest of the United States in the dispute with Venezuela, on the ground that Venezuela was one of the nations of the Western Hemisphere. This concession practically involved recognition of the interest of the United States in case of future disputes with other American powers. The arbitration treaty thus arranged between Great Britain and Venezuela under the auspices of the United States submitted the whole disputed area to judicial decision but adopted the rule that fifty years of occupation should give a sufficient title for possession. The arbitration tribunal, which met in Paris in 1899, decided on a division of the disputed territory but found that the claim of Great Britain was, on the whole, more nearly correct than that of Venezuela.

Cleveland's startling and unconventional method of dealing with this controversy has been explained by all kinds of conjectures. For example, it has been charged that his message was the product of a fishing trip on which whisky flowed too freely; on the other hand, it has been asserted that the message was an astute political play for the thunder of patriotic applause. More seriously, Cleveland has been charged by one set of critics with bluffing, and by another with recklessly running the risk of war on a trivial provocation. The charge of bluffing comes nearer the fact, for President Cleveland probably had never a moment's doubt that the forces making for peace between the two nations would be victorious. If he may be said to have thrown a bomb, he certainly had attached a safety valve to it, for the investigation which he proposed could not but give time for the passions produced by his message to cool. It is interesting to note in passing that delay for investigation was a device which that other great Democrat, William Jennings Bryan, Cleveland's greatest political enemy, sought, during his short term as Secretary of State under President Wilson, to make universal in a series of arbitration treaties — treaties which now bind the United States and many other countries, how tightly no man can tell.

While, however, Cleveland's action was based rather on a belief in peace than on an expectation of war, it cannot be dismissed as merely a bluff. Not only was he convinced that the principle involved was worth establishing whatever the cost might be, but he was certain that the method he employed was the only one which could succeed, for in no other way was it possible to wake England to a realization of the fact that the United States was full-grown and imbued with a new consciousness of its strength. So far was Cleveland's message from provoking war that it caused the people of Great Britain vitally to realize for the first time the importance of friendship with the United States. It marks a change in their attitude toward things American which found expression not only in diplomacy, but in various other ways, and which strikingly revealed itself in the international politics of the next few years. Not that hostility was converted into affection, but a former condescension gave way to an appreciative friendliness towards the people of the United States.

The reaction in America was somewhat different. Cleveland had united the country upon a matter of foreign policy, not completely, it is true, but to a greater degree than Blaine had ever succeeded in doing. More important than this unity of feeling throughout the land, however, was the development of a spirit of inquiry among the people. Suddenly confronted by changes of policy that might bring wealth or poverty, life or death, the American people began to take the foreign relations of the United States more seriously than they had since the days of the Napoleonic wars. Yet it is not surprising that when the Venezuela difficulty had been settled and Secretary Olney and Sir Julian Pauncefote, the British Ambassador, had concluded a general treaty of arbitration, the Senate should have rejected it, for the lesson that caution was necessary in international affairs had been driven home. Time was needed for the new generation to formulate its foreign policy.

# CHAPTER VII

### THE OUTBREAK OF THE WAR WITH SPAIN

BEFORE the nineteenth century ended, the Samoan, Hawaiian, and Venezuelan episodes had done much to quicken a national consciousness in the people of the United States and at the same time to break down their sense of isolation from the rest of the world. Commerce and trade were also important factors in overcoming this traditional isolation. Not only was American trade growing, but it was changing in character. Argentina was beginning to compete with the United States in exporting wheat and meat, while American manufacturers were reaching the point where they were anxious for foreign markets in which they felt they could compete with the products of Great Britain and Germany.

In a thousand ways and without any loss of vigor the sense of American nationality was expressing itself. The study of American history was introduced into the lower schools, and a new group of historians began scientifically to investigate whence the American people had come and what they really were. In England, such popular movements find instant expression in literature; in the United States they take the form of societies. Innumerable patriotic organizations such as the "Daughters of the American Revolution" and a host of others, sought to trace out American genealogy and to perpetuate the memory of American military and naval achievements. Respect for the American flag was taught in schools, and the question was debated as to whether its use in comic opera indicated respect or insult. This new nationalism was unlike the expansionist movement of the fifties in that it laid no particular stress upon the incorporation of the neighboring republics by a process of federation. On the whole, the people had lost their faith in the assimilating influence of republican institutions and did not desire to annex alien territory and races. They were now more concerned with the consolidation of their own country and with its place in the world. Nor were they as neglectful as their fathers had been of the material means by which to accomplish their somewhat indefinite purposes.

The reconstruction of the American Navy, which

had attained such magnitude and played so important a part in the Civil War but which had been allowed to sink into the merest insignificance, was begun by William E. Chandler, the Secretary of the Navy under President Arthur. William C. Whitney, his successor under President Cleveland, continued the work with energy. Captain Alfred T. Mahan began in 1883 to publish that series of studies in naval history which won him world-wide recognition and did so much to revolutionize prevailing conceptions of naval strategy. A Naval War College was established in 1884, at Newport, Rhode Island where naval officers could continue the studies which they had begun at Annapolis.

The total neglect of the army was not entirely the result of indifference. The experience with volunteers in the Civil War had given almost universal confidence that the American people could constitute themselves an army at will. The presence of several heroes of that war in succession in the position of commander-in-chief of the army had served to diffuse a sense of security among the people. Here and there military drill was introduced in school and college, but the regular army attracted none of the romantic interest that clung about the navy, and the militia was almost totally neglected. Individual officers, such as young Lieutenant Tasker Bliss, began to study the new technique of warfare which was to make fighting on land as different from that of the wars of Napoleon as naval warfare was different from that of the time of Nelson. Yet in spite of obviously changing conditions, no provision was made for the encouragement of young army officers in advanced and up-to-date studies. While their contemporaries in other professions were adding graduate training to the general education which a college gave, the graduates of West Point were considered to have made themselves in four years sufficiently proficient for all the purposes of warfare.

By the middle nineties thoughtful students of contemporary movements were aware that a new epoch in national history was approaching. What form this national development would take was, however, still uncertain, and some great event was obviously required to fix its character. Blaine's Pan-Americanism had proved insufficient and, though the baiting of Great Britain was welcome to a vociferous minority, the forces making for peace were stronger than those in favor of war. Whatever differences there were did not reach to fundamentals but were rather in the nature of legal disputes between neighbors whom a real emergency would quickly bring to the assistance of each other. A crisis involving interest, propinquity, and sentiment, was needed to shake the nation into an activity which would clear its views.

At the very time of the Venezuela difficulty, such a crisis was taking shape in the Caribbean. Cuba had always been an object of immediate concern to the United States. The statesmen of the Jeffersonian period all looked to its eventually becoming part of American territory. Three quarters of a century before, when the revolt of the Spanish colonies had halted on the shores of the mainland, leaving the rich island of Cuba untouched, John Quincy Adams, on April 28, 1823, in a lengthy and long-considered dispatch to Mr. Nelson, the American Minister to Spain, asserted that the United States could not consent to the passing of Cuba from the flag of Spain to that of any other European power, that under existing conditions Cuba was considered safer in the hands of Spain than in those of the revolutionaries, and that the United States stood for the maintenance of the *status quo*, with the expectation that Cuba would ultimately become American territory.

By the late forties and the fifties, however, the

times had changed, and American policy had changed with them. It was becoming more and more evident that, although no real revolution had as yet broken out, the "Pearl of the Antilles" was bound to Spain by compulsion rather than by love. In the United States there was a general feeling that the time had at last come to realize the vision of Jefferson and Adams and to annex Cuba. But the complications of the slavery question prevented immediate annexation. As a slave colony which might become a slave state, the South wanted Cuba, but the majority in the North did not.

After the Civil War in the United States was over, revolution at length flared forth in 1868, from end to end of the island. Sympathy with the Cubans was widespread in the United States. The hand of the Government, however, was stayed by recent history. Americans felt keenly the right of governments to exert their full strength to put down rebellion, for they themselves were prosecuting against Great Britain a case based on what they contended was her too lax enforcement of her obligations to the American Government and on the assistance which she had given to the South. The great issue determined the lesser, and for ten years the United States watched the Cuban revolution without taking part in it, but not, however, without protest and remonstrance. Claiming special rights as a close and necessarily interested neighbor, the United States constantly made suggestions as to the manner of the contest and its settlement. Some of these Spain grudgingly allowed, and it was in part by American insistence that slavery was finally abolished in the island. Further internal reform, however, was not the wish and was perhaps beyond the power of Spain. Although the revolution was seemingly brought to a close in 1878, its embers continued to smolder for nearly a score of years until in 1895 they again burst into flame.

War in Cuba could not help affecting in a very intimate way the people of the United States. They bought much the greater part of the chief Cuban crops, sugar and tobacco. American capital had been invested in the island, particularly in plantations. For years Cubans of liberal tendencies had sent their sons to be educated in the United States, very many of whom had been naturalized before returning home. Cuba was but ninety miles from Florida, and much of our coastwise shipping passed in sight of the island. The people of the United States were aroused to sympathy and to a desire to be of assistance when they saw that the Cubans, so near geographically and so bound to them by many commercial ties, were engaged against a foreign monarchy in a struggle for freedom and a republican form of government. Ethan Allen headed a Cuban committee in New York and by his historic name associated the new revolution with the memory of the American struggle for freedom. The Cuban flag was displayed in the United States, Cuban bonds were sold, and volunteers and arms were sent to the aid of the insurgents.

Owing to the nature of the country and the character of the people, a Cuban revolution had its peculiarities. The island is a very long and rugged mountain chain surrounded by fertile, cultivated plains. The insurgents from their mountain refuges spied out the land, pounced upon unprotected spots, burned crops and sugar mills, and were off before troops could arrive. The portion of the population in revolt at any particular time was rarely large. Many were insurgents one week and peaceful citizens the next. The fact that the majority of the population sympathized with the insurgents enabled the latter to melt into the landscape without leaving a sign. A provisional government hurried on mule-back from place to place. The Spanish Government, contrary to custom, acted at this time with some energy: it put two hundred thousand soldiers into the island; it raised large levies of loyal Cubans; it was almost always victorious; yet the revolution would not down. Martínez Campos, the "Pacificator" of the first revolution, was this time unable to protect the plains. In 1896 he was replaced by General Weyler, who undertook a new system. He started to corral the insurgents by a chain of blockhouses and barbed wire fences from ocean to sea — the first completely guarded cross-country line since the frontier walls of the Roman Empire in Europe and the Great Wall of China in Asia. He then proceeded to starve out the insurgents by destroying all the food in the areas to which they were confined. As the revolutionists lived largely on the pillage of plantations in their neighborhood, this policy involved the destruction of the crops of the loyal as well as of the disloyal, of Americans as well as of Cubans. The population of the devastated plantations was gathered into *reconcentrado* camps where, penned promiscuously into small reservations, they were entirely dependent upon a Government which was poor in supplies and as careless of sanitation as it was of humanity. The camps became pest holes, spreading contagion to all regions having intercourse with Cuba, and in vain the interned victims were crying aloud for succor.

This new policy of disregard for property and life deeply involved American interests and sensibilities. The State Department maintained that Spain was responsible for the destruction of American property by insurgents. This Spain denied, for, while she never officially recognized the insurgents as belligerents, the insurrection had passed beyond her control. This was, indeed, the position which the Spanish Treaty Claims Commission subsequently took in ruling that to establish a claim it would be necessary to show that the destruction of property was the consequence of negligence upon the part of Spanish authorities or of military orders. Of other serious grievances there was no doubt. American citizens were imprisoned, interned in *reconcentrado* camps, and otherwise maltreated. The nationality of American sufferers was in some cases disputed, and the necessity of dealing with each of these doubtful cases by the slow and roundabout method of complaint to Madrid, which referred matters back to Havana, which reported to Madrid, served but to add irritation to delay. American resentment, too, was fired by the sufferings of the Cubans themselves as much as by the losses and difficulties of American citizens.

One change of extreme importance had taken place since the Cuban revolt of 1868–78. This was the development of the modern American newspaper. It was no longer possible for the people at large to remain ignorant of what was taking place at their very doors. Correspondents braved the yellow fever and imprisonment in order to furnish the last details of each new horror. Foremost in this work were William Randolph Hearst, who made new records of sensationalism in his papers, particularly in the New York *Journal*, and Joseph Pulitzer, proprietor of the New York *World*. Hearst is reported to have said that it cost him three millions to bring on the Spanish American War. The net result of all this newspaper activity was that it became impossible for the American people to remain in happy ignorance of what was going on in the world. Their reaction to the facts was their own.

President Cleveland modeled his policy upon that of Grant and Grant's Secretary, Hamilton

Fish. He did not recognize the independence of the Cuban republic, for that would have meant immediate war with Spain; nor did he recognize even its belligerency. Public men in the United States were still convinced that Great Britain had erred in recognizing the belligerency of the Southern Confederacy, and consistency of foreign policy demanded that the Government should not accord recognition to a Government without a navy, a capital, or fixed territory. This decision made it particularly difficult for the President to perform his acknowledged duty to Spain, of preventing aid being sent from the United States to the insurgents. He issued the proper proclamations, and American officials were reasonably diligent, it is true, but without any of the special powers which would have resulted from a recognized state of war they were unable to prevent a leakage of supplies. As a result General Weyler had some ground for saying, though with characteristic Spanish extravagance, that it was American aid which gave life to the revolt.

President Cleveland energetically pressed all cases involving American rights; he offered mediation; he remonstrated against the cruelty of Weyler's methods; he pointed out that the United

States could not forever allow an island so near and so closely related to be in flames without intervention. Spain, however, assumed a rather lofty tone, and Cleveland was able to accomplish nothing. Senator Lodge and other Republicans violently attacked his policy as procrastinating, and the nation as a whole looked forward with interest to the approaching change in administration.

William McKinley, who became President on March 4, 1897, was not actively interested in foreign affairs. This he illustrated in a striking way by appointing as Secretary of State John Sherman of Ohio, a man of undoubtedly high ability but one whose whole reputation rested upon his financial leadership, and who now, at the age of seventy-four, was known to be incapacitated for vigorous action. To the very moment of crisis, McKinley was opposed to a war with Spain; he was opposed to the form of the declaration of war and he was opposed to the terms of peace which ended the war. Emphatically not a leader, he was, however, unsurpassed in his day as a reader of public opinion, and he believed his function to be that of interpreting the national mind. Nor did he yield his opinion in a grudging manner. He grasped broadly the consequences of each new position which the public assumed, and he was a master at securing harmonious coöperation for a desired end.

The platform of the Republican party had declared: "The Government of Spain having lost control of Cuba, and being unable to protect the property or lives of resident American citizens, or to comply with its treaty obligations, we believe that the Government of the United States should actively use its influence and good offices to restore peace and give independence to the island." With this mandate, McKinley sought to free Cuba, absolutely or practically, while at the same time maintaining peace with Spain. On June 26, 1897, Secretary Sherman sent a note to the Spanish Minister, protesting against the Spanish methods of war and asserting that "the inclusion of a thousand or more of our own citizens among the victims of this policy" gives "the President the right of specific remonstrance, but in the just fulfillment of his duty he cannot limit himself to these formal grounds of complaint. He is bound by the higher obligation of his representative office to protest against the uncivilized and inhuman conduct of the campaign in the island of Cuba. He conceives that he has a right to demand that a war, conducted almost within sight of our shores and grievously affecting American citizens and their interests throughout the length and breadth of the land, shall at least be conducted according to the military codes of civilization.''

Negotiations between the United States and Spain have always been peculiarly irritating, owing to temperamental differences between the two peoples. McKinley, however, had in mind a program for which there was some hope of success. He was willing to agree to some form of words which would leave Spain in titular possession of the island, thereby making a concession to Spanish pride, for he knew that Spain was always more loath to surrender the form than the substance. This hope of the President was strengthened, towards the end of 1897, by a dramatic incident in the political life of Spain. On the 8th of August, the Spanish Prime Minister, the Conservative Antonio Cánovas del Castillo, was assassinated, and was succeeded on the 4th of October by the Liberal, Praxédes Mateo Sagasta.

The new Spanish Government listened to American demands and made large promises of amelioration of conditions in Cuba. General Blanco was substituted for General Weyler, whose cruelty had made him known in the American press as "the

Butcher"; it was announced that the *reconcentrado* camps would be broken up; and the Queen Regent decreed the legislative autonomy of Cuba. Arrangements had been made for the handling of minor disputes directly with the Governor-General of Cuba through the American Consul General at Havana, General Fitzhugh Lee. On December 6, 1897, McKinley, in his annual message to Congress, counseled patience. Convinced of the good intentions of the new Spanish Government, he sought to induce American public sentiment to allow it time to act. He continued nevertheless to urge upon Spain the fact that in order to be effective action must be prompt.

Public sentiment against Spain grew every day stronger in the United States and was given startling impulse in February, 1898, by two of those critical incidents which are almost sure to occur when general causes are potent enough to produce a white heat of popular feeling. The Spanish Minister in the United States, Señor Dupuy de Lôme, had aroused the suspicion, during his summer residence on the north shore of Massachusetts Bay, that he was collecting information which would be useful to a Spanish fleet operating on that coast. Whether this charge was true or not, at any

rate he wrote a letter to a friend, a Madrid editor
visiting Havana, in which he characterized Mc-
Kinley as a vacillating and timeserving politician.
Alert American newspaper men, who practically
constituted a secret service of some efficiency, man-
aged to obtain the letter. On February 9, 1898,
De Lôme saw a facsimile of this letter printed in
a newspaper and at once cabled his resignation.
In immediately accepting De Lôme's resignation
Spain anticipated an American demand for his
recall and thus saved Spanish pride, though undoubtedly at the expense of additional irritation in
the United States, where it was thought that he
should have been punished instead of being allowed
to slip away.

Infinitely more serious than this diplomatic
*faux pas* was the disaster which befell the United
States battleship *Maine*. On January 24, 1898,
the Government had announced its intention of
sending a warship on a friendly visit to Havana,
with the desire of impressing the local Cuban authorities with the imminence of American power.
Not less important was the purpose of affording
protection to American citizens endangered by the
rioting of Spaniards, who were angry because they
believed that Sagasta by his conciliatory policy was

betraying the interests of Spain. Accordingly the *Maine*, commanded by Captain Sigsbee, was dispatched to Cuba and arrived on the 25th of January in the harbor of Havana. On the night of the 15th of February, an explosion utterly wrecked the vessel and killed 260 of the crew, besides wounding ninety.

The responsibility for this calamity has never been positively determined. It may have resulted from an accidental internal explosion, from the official action of the Spanish authorities, from the unofficial zeal of subordinate Spanish officers, or even — as suggested by Speaker Reed who was an opponent of war — by action of the insurgents themselves with the purpose of embroiling the United States and Spain. The careful investigations which were afterwards made brought to light evidence of both internal and external explosions; it therefore seems probable that an external mine was the prime cause of the disaster and that the internal explosion followed as a consequence. No direct evidence has been discovered which would fix the responsibility for the placing of the mine, but it is reasonable to attribute it to the Spanish hotheads of Havana. It is not impossible that the insurgents were responsible; but it is incredible that the Spanish Government planned the explosion.

The hasty, though perhaps natural, conclusion to which American public sentiment at once leaped, however, was that the disaster was the work of Spain, without making any discrimination between the Government itself and the disaffected factions. A general sorrow and anger throughout the United States reinforced the popular anxiety for national interests and the humane regard for the Cubans. Press and public oratory demanded official action. "Remember the Maine!" was an admonition which everywhere met the eye and ear. The venerable and trusted Senator Proctor, who visited Cuba, came back with the report that conditions on the island were intolerable. On the 9th of March, "Uncle Joe" Cannon, the watchdog of the Treasury, introduced a bill appropriating fifty million dollars to be used for national defense at the discretion of the President. No doubt remained in the public mind that war would result unless the withdrawal of Spanish authority from Cuba could be arranged peaceably and immediately.

Even in this final stage of the negotiations it is sufficiently obvious that the United States Government was particularly desirous of preserving peace.

There is also little doubt that the Spanish Government in good faith had the same desire. The intelligent classes in Spain realized that the days of Spanish rule in Cuba were practically over. The Liberals believed that, under the circumstances, war with the United States would be a misfortune. Many of the Conservatives, however, believed that a war, even if unsuccessful, was the only way of saving the dynasty, and that the dynasty was worth saving. Public opinion in Spain was therefore no less inflamed than in America, but it was less well-informed. Cartoons represented the American hog, which would readily fall before the Spanish rapier accustomed to its nobler adversary the bull. Spanish pride, impervious to facts and statistics, would brook no supine submission on the part of its people to foreign demands. It was a question how far the Spanish Government could bring itself to yield points in season which it fully realized must be yielded in the end.

The negotiation waxed too hot for the aged John Sherman, and was conducted by the Assistant Secretary, William Rufus Day, a close friend of the President, but a man comparatively unknown to the public. When Day officially succeeded

Sherman (April 26, 1898) he had to face as fierce a light of publicity as ever beat upon a public man in the United States. Successively in charge of the Cuban negotiations, Secretary of State from April to September, 1898, President of the Paris Peace Commission in October, in December, after a career of prime national importance for nine months in which he had demonstrated his high competence, Day retired to the relative obscurity of the United States circuit bench. Although later raised to the Supreme Court, he has never since been a national figure. As an example of a meteoric career of a man of solid rather than meteoric qualities, his case is unparalleled in American history.

The acting Secretary of State telegraphed the ultimatum of the Government on March 27, 1898, to General Stewart L. Woodford, then Minister to Spain. By the terms of this document, in the first place there was to be an immediate amnesty which would last until the 1st of October and during which Spain would communicate with the insurgents through the President of the United States; in the second place, the *reconcentrado* policy was to cease immediately, and relief for the suffering Cubans was to be admitted from the

United States. Then, if satisfactory terms were not reached by the 1st of October, the President was to be recognized as arbiter between the Spaniards and the insurgents.

On the 30th of March, Spain abrogated the *reconcentrado* policy in the "western provinces of Cuba," and on the following day offered to arbitrate the questions arising out of the sinking of the *Maine.* On Sunday, the 3d of April, a cablegram from General Woodford was received by the State Department indicating that Spain was seeking a formula for an armistice that should not too obviously appear to be submission and suggesting that the President ask the Pope to intervene and that the United States abstain from all show of force. "If you can still give me time and reasonable liberty of action," ran Woodford's message, "I will get you the peace you desire so much and for which you have labored so hard." To this the Secretary of State immediately replied that the President would not ask the intervention of the Pope, and that the Government would use the fleet as it saw fit. "Would the peace you are so confident of securing," asked the Secretary, "mean the independence of Cuba? The President cannot hold his message longer than Tuesday."

On Tuesday, the 5th of April, General Woodford cabled:

Should the Queen proclaim the following before twelve o'clock noon of Wednesday, April 6th, will you sustain the Queen, and can you prevent hostile action by Congress? "At the request of the Holy Father, in this Passion Week and in the name of Christ, I proclaim immediate and unconditional suspension of hostilities in the island of Cuba. This suspension is to become immediately effective as soon as accepted by the insurgents of that island, and is to continue for the space of six months to the 5th day of October, 1898. I do this to give time for passions to cease, and in the sincere hope and belief that during this suspension permanent and honorable peace may be obtained between the insular government of Cuba and those of my subjects in that island who are now in rebellion against the authority of Spain. . . ." Please read this in the light of all my previous telegrams and letters. I believe this means peace, which the sober judgment of our people will approve long before next November, and which must be approved at the bar of final history.

To this message the Secretary of State replied:

The President highly appreciates the Queen's desire for peace. He cannot assume to influence the action of the American Congress beyond a discharge of his constitutional duty in transmitting the whole matter to them with such recommendations as he deems necessary and expedient.

On the 9th of April the Queen granted the amnesty, on the formula of a request by the European powers. On the next day, General Woodford cabled that the United States could obtain for Cuba a satisfactory autonomy, or independence, or the cession of the island.

It was evident that there was no difference of opinion among those in authority in the United States as to the fact that Cuba must be severed from Spain. There were, however, differences of judgment as to which of the three methods suggested by Woodford was preferable, and there was a substantial disagreement as to the means necessary to realize the aims of the American Government. General Woodford believed that Spain would grant the demands of the United States, if she were given time and were not pressed to the point of endangering her dignity. The overwhelming majority in Congress, and particularly the leaders of the dominant Republican party with the exception of Speaker Reed, refused to believe in the sincerity of the Spanish Government. The Administration could not overlook the fact that the Spanish Government, however sincere it might be, might not be able to execute its promises. Great Britain had just recognized the United States as intermediary in a dispute between herself and one of the American nations. Spain, in a dispute much more serious to the United States, refused publicly to admit American intervention, while she did recognize that of the Pope and the European powers. Was it then possible that a Government which was either unwilling or afraid openly to acknowledge American interest in April would, by October, yield to the wishes of the Administration? Was it certain or likely that if the Spanish Government did so yield, it would remain in power?

Reluctantly President McKinley decided that he could not announce to Congress that he had secured the acceptance of the American policy. In his message to Congress on the 11th of April, he reviewed the negotiation and concluded by recommending forcible intervention. On the 19th of April, Congress, by joint resolution, called upon Spain to withdraw from Cuba and authorized the President to use force to compel her to do so. Congress, however, was not content to leave the future of the island merely indefinite, but added that the United States did not desire Cuba and that the "people of the island of Cuba are, and of right ought to be, free and independent." This decision ruled out both autonomy and cession as solutions of the problem. It put an end to the American century-long dream of annexing Cuba, unless the people of the island themselves desired such a relation; and it practically determined the recognition of the unstable Cuban Government then in existence. This decision on the part of Congress, however, reflected the deep-seated conviction of the American people regarding freedom and plainly put the issue where the popular majority wished it to be — upon a basis of unselfish sympathy with struggling neighbors.

The resolution was signed by the President on the 20th of April. On the following day, Admiral Sampson's fleet left Key West with orders to blockade the coast of Cuba, and, in the absence of a formal declaration of war, this strategic move may be considered as its actual beginning. On the 25th of April, Congress declared "that war be, and the same is hereby, declared to exist, and that war has existed since the twenty-first of April, Anno Domini, eighteen hundred and ninety-eight, including the said day, between the United States of America and the Kingdom of Spain."

# CHAPTER VIII

## DEWEY AND MANILA BAY

WAR had begun, but the majority of the American people had hardly considered seriously how they were to fight. Fortunately their navy already existed, and it was upon it that they had to rely in the opening moments of hostility. Ton for ton, gun for gun, it stood on fairly even terms with that of Spain. Captain, later Admiral, Mahan, considered that the loss of the *Maine* shifted a slight paper advantage from the United States to Spain. In personnel, however, the American Navy soon proved its overwhelming superiority, which was due not solely to innate ability but also to sound professional training.

The Secretary of the Navy, John D. Long, had a thorough appreciation of values. Although Congress had not provided for a general staff, he himself appointed a Naval War Board, which served many of the same purposes. Upon this Board he

appointed Rear Admiral Sicard, who but for ill
health would have commanded the main fleet;
Captain A. S. Crowninshield; and, most important,
Captain A. T. Mahan, whose equal as master of
the theory and history of naval warfare no navy
of the world could show. The spirit of the fighting
force was speedily exhibited by such exploits as
that of Lieutenant Victor Blue in boldly plunging
into the Cuban wilderness to obtain information
regarding the position of Admiral Cervera's fleet,
though in this dangerous sort of work the individual palm must be given to Lieutenant A. S. Rowan
of the army, whose energy and initiative in overcoming obstacles are immortalized in Elbert Hub-
bard's *Message to Garcia*, the best American parable
of efficient service since the days of Franklin.

Efficient, however, as was the navy, it was far
from being a complete fighting force. Its fighting
vessels were totally unsupplied with that cloud of
servers — colliers, mother ships, hospital ships, and
scouts — which we now know must accompany a
fleet. The merchant marine, then at almost its
lowest point, was not in a position entirely to fill
the need. The United States had no extensive
store of munitions. Over all operations there hung
a cloud of uncertainty. Except for the short

campaign of the Chino-Japanese War of 1894, modern implements of sea war remained untested. Scientific experiment, valuable and necessary as it was, did not carry absolute conviction regarding efficient service. Would the weapons of offense or defense prove most effective? Accidents on shipboard and even the total destruction of vessels had been common to all navies during times of peace. That the *Maine* had not been a victim of the failure of her own mechanism was not then certain. Such misgivings were in the minds of many officers. Indeed, a report of the total disappearance of two battling fleets would not have found the watchful naval experts of the world absolutely incredulous. So much the higher, therefore, was the heroism of those who led straight to battle that complex and as yet unproved product of the brain — the modern warship.

While negotiations with Spain were in their last stages, at the orders of Secretary Long a swift vessel left San Francisco for Honolulu. There its precious cargo was transferred to the warship *Baltimore*, which then made hurriedly for Hongkong. It contained the ammunition which was absolutely necessary if Commodore George Dewey, in command of the Asiatic squadron, was to play a part in

the war. The position of his squadron, eve[...]
it received its ammunition, was indeed singu[...]
After the war began, it was unable to obtain coal
or other supplies from any neutral port and at
the same time it was equally unable to remain in
any such port without being interned for the duration of the war. There remained but one course
of action. It must not be forgotten that the Spanish empire stretched eastward as well as westward.
Already William Pitt, when he had foreseen in
1760 the entrance of Spain into the war which England was then waging with France, had planned
expeditions against both Cuba and the Philippines.
Now in 1898 the Navy Department of the United
States, anticipating war, saw in the proximity of
the American squadron to the Spanish islands
of the Philippines an opportunity rather than a
problem. Commodore George Dewey, the commander of the Asiatic squadron, was fully prepared
to enter into the plan. As early as the seventies,
when the *Virginius* affair[1] threatened war between

---

[1] A dispute between the United States and Spain, arising out of the
capture of the *Virginius*, an American vessel engaged in filibustering
off the coast of Cuba, and the execution at Santiago of the captain
and a number of the crew and passengers. The vessel and the sur-
viving passengers were finally restored by the Spanish authorities, who
agreed to punish the officials responsible for the illegal acts.

and the United States, Dewey, then a commander on the west coast of Mexico, had proposed, in case war were declared, that he sail for the Philippines and capture Manila. Now he was prepared to seek in the hostile ports of those islands the liberty that international law forbade him in the neutral ports of Asia. How narrow a margin of time he had in which to make this bold stroke may be realized from the fact that the *Baltimore*, his second vessel in size, reached Hongkong on the 22d of April and went into dry dock on the 23d, and that on the following day the squadron was ordered either to leave the port or to intern.

The little armada of six vessels with which Dewey started for the Philippines was puny enough from the standpoint of today; yet it was strong enough to cope with the larger but more old-fashioned Spanish fleet, or with the harbor defenses unless these included mines — of whose absence Dewey was at the moment unaware. If, however, the Spanish commander could unite the strength of his vessels and that of the coast defenses, Dewey might find it impossible to destroy the Spanish fleet. In that case, the plight of the American squadron would be precarious, if its ultimate self-destruction or internment did not become necessary.

Commodore Dewey belonged to that school of American naval officers who combine the spirit of Farragut's "Damn the torpedoes" with a thorough knowledge of the latest scientific devices. Though he would take all precautions, he would not allow the unknown to hold him back. After a brief rendezvous for tuning up at Mirs Bay near Hongkong on the Chinese coast, Dewey steered straight for Subig Bay in the Philippines, where he expected to meet his opponent. Finding the Bay empty, he steamed on without pause and entered the Boca Grande, the southern channel leading to Manila Bay, at midnight of the 30th of April. Slowly, awaiting daylight, but steadily he approached Manila. Coming within three miles of the city, he discovered the Spanish fleet, half a dozen miles to the southeast, at the naval station of Cavité. Still without a pause, the American squadron moved to the attack.

The Spanish Admiral Montojo tried, though ineffectually, to come to close quarters, for his guns were of smaller caliber than those of the American ships, but he was forced to keep his vessels for the most part in line between the Americans and the shore. Commodore Dewey sailed back and forth five times, raking the Spanish ships and the shore batteries with his fire. Having guns of longer range than those of the Spaniards, he could have kept out of their fire and slowly hammered them to pieces; but he preferred a closer position where he could use more guns and therefore do quicker work. How well he was justified in taking this risk is shown by the fact that no man was killed on the American fleet that day and only a few were wounded. After a few hours' fighting, with a curious interval when the Americans withdrew and breakfasted, Dewey completed the destruction or capture of the Spanish fleet, and found himself the victor with his own ships uninjured and in full fighting trim. By the 3d of May, the naval station at Cavité and the batteries at the entrance of Manila Bay were in the hands of Commodore Dewey, and the Asiatic squadron had wrested a safe and commodious harbor from the enemy.

Secure for the moment and free, Dewey found himself in as precarious a strategic position as has ever confronted a naval officer. With his six war vessels and 1707 men, he was unsupported and at least a month's voyage from America. It was two months, indeed, before any American troops or additional ships reached him. Meanwhile the Spaniards held Manila, and a Spanish fleet, formidable under the circumstances, began to sail for the Philippines. Nevertheless Dewey proceeded to blockade Manila, which was besieged on the land side by the Filipino insurgents under Aguinaldo. This siege was indeed an advantage to the Americans as it distressed the enemy and gave an opportunity to obtain supplies from the mainland. Dewey, however, placed no confidence in Aguinaldo, and further was instructed by Secretary Long on the 26th of May as follows: "It is desirable, as far as possible, and consistent for your success and safety, not to have political alliances with the insurgents or any faction in the islands that would incur liability to maintain their cause in the future." Meanwhile foreign nations were rushing vessels to this critical spot in the Pacific. On the 17th of June, Dewey sent a cable, which had to be relayed to Hongkong by boat, reporting that there were collected, in Manila Bay, a French and a Japanese warship, two British, and three German. Another German man-of-war was expected, which would make the German squadron as strong as the American.

The presence of so large a German force, it was felt, could hardly fail to have definite significance, and therefore caused an anxiety at home which would, indeed, have been all the keener had Admiral Dewey not kept many of his troubles to himself. European sympathy was almost wholly with Spain. The French, for instance, had invested heavily in Spanish bonds, many of which were secured on the Cuban revenues. There was also perhaps some sense of solidarity among the Latin races in Europe and a feeling that the United States was a colossus willfully exerting itself against a weak antagonist. It was not likely that this feeling was strong enough to lead to action, but at least during that summer of 1898 it was somewhat unpleasant for American tourists in Paris, and an untoward episode might easily have brought unfriendly sentiment to a dangerous head. Austria had never been very friendly to the United States, particularly since the execution of the Emperor Maximilian in Mexico, which his brother Francis Joseph believed the United States could have prevented, and was tied to Spain by the fact that the Queen Regent was an Austrian Hapsburg.

It was evident, moreover, that in Europe there was a vague but nevertheless real dread of the economic potentialities of the United States — a fear which led, in the next few years, to the suggestion that the American invasion of trade should be resisted by a general European economic organization which would even overrule the natural tendency of powers to group themselves into hostile camps. In 1898 it seemed possible that the United States was consciously planning to become a world military power also, and a feeling, not exactly like Blaine's "America for the Americans" but rather of "the world for Europeans," gathered force to meet any attempt at American expansion.

Even before war had broken out between Spain and the United States, this sentiment had sufficiently crystallized to result in a not quite usual diplomatic action. On April 6, 1898, the representatives of Great Britain, Germany, France, Austro-Hungary, Russia, and Italy, presented a note to the Government of the United States making "a pressing appeal to the feelings of humanity and moderation of the President and of the American people in their differences with Spain. They earnestly hope that further negotiations will lead to an agreement which, while securing the maintenance of peace, will afford all necessary guarantees for the reëstablishment of order in Cuba."

Of all the European powers none was more interested than Germany in the situation in the Western Hemisphere. There seems to be no doubt that the Kaiser made the remark to an Englishman with reference to the Spanish American War: "If I had had a larger fleet I would have taken Uncle Sam by the scruff of his neck." Though the reason for Germany's attitude has never been proven by documents, circumstantial evidence points convincingly to the explanation. The quest for a colonial empire, upon which Bismarck had embarked rather reluctantly and late, had been taken up with feverish zeal by William II, his successor in the direction of German policy. Not content with the commercial conquests which German trade was making in all countries of the earth, the Kaiser wanted a place in the sun exclusively his own. The world seemed, however, as firmly closed to the late-comer in search of colonies as it was open to him as the bearer of cheap and useful goods. Such remnants of territory as lay on the counter he quickly seized, but they hardly made an empire.

It is not, therefore, a daring conjecture that the Kaiser was as carefully watching the decrepit empire of Spain as he was the traditional sick man of Europe, the empire of Turkey. In 1898 revolutions were sapping both the extremities of the Spanish dominions. The Kaiser, while he doubtless realized that Cuba would not fall to him, in all probability expected that he would be able to get the Philippines. Certain it is that at the close of the Spanish American War he bought all the remaining Spanish possessions in the Pacific. If such had been his expectations with regard to the Philippines, the news of Dewey's victory must have brought him a bitter disappointment, while at the same time the careless and indiscreet remark of an American official to certain Germans — "We don't want the Philippines; why don't you take them?" — may well have given him a feeling that perhaps the question was still open.

Under such circumstances, with Europe none too well-disposed and the Kaiser watching events with a jealous eye, it was very important to the United States not to be without a friend. In England sympathy for America ran strong and deep. The British Government was somewhat in alarm over the political solitude in which Great Britain found herself, even though its head, Lord Salisbury, described the position as one of "splendid isolation." The unexpected reaction of friendliness on the part of Great Britain which had followed the Venezuela affair continued to augment, and relations between the two countries were kept smooth by the new American Ambassador, John Hay, whom Queen Victoria described as "the most interesting of all the ambassadors I have known." More important still, in Great Britain alone was there a public who appreciated the real sentiment of humanity underlying the entrance of the United States into the war with Spain; and this public actually had some weight in politics. The people of both Great Britain and the United States were easily moved to respond with money and personal service to the cry of suffering anywhere in the world. Just before the Spanish American War, Gladstone had made his last great campaign protesting against the new massacres in Armenia; and in the United States the Republican platform of 1896 had declared that "the massacres in Armenia have aroused the deep sympathy and just indignation of the American people, and we believe that the United States should exercise all the influence it can properly exert to bring these atrocities to an end."

John Hay wrote to Henry Cabot Lodge, of the Senate Committee on Foreign Affairs, April 5, 1898, as follows: "For the first time in my life I find the drawing-room sentiment altogether with us. If we wanted it — which, of course, we do not — we could have the practical assistance of the British

Navy — on the *do ut des* principle, naturally."
On the 25th of May he added: "It is a moment of immense importance, not only for the present, but for all the future. It is hardly too much to say the interests of civilization are bound up in the direction the relations of England and America are to take in the next few months." Already on the 15th of May, Joseph Chamberlain, the Colonial Secretary, had said to the Birmingham Liberal Unionists: "What is our next duty? It is to establish and to maintain bonds of permanent amity with our kinsmen across the Atlantic. There is a powerful and a generous nation. . . . Their laws, their literature, their standpoint upon every question are the same as ours."

In Manila Harbor, where Dewey lay with his squadron, these distant forces of European colonial policy were at work. The presence of representative foreign warships to observe the maintenance of the blockade was a natural and usual naval circumstance. The arrival of two German vessels therefore caused no remark, although they failed to pay the usual respects to the blockading squadron. On the 12th of May a third arrived and created some technical inconvenience by being commanded by an officer who outranked Commodore Dewey.

A German transport which was in the harbor made the total number of German personnel superior to that of the Americans, and the arrival of the *Kaiser* on the 12th of June gave the Germans distinct naval preponderance.

The presence of so powerful a squadron in itself closely approached an international discourtesy. Disregarding the laws of blockade, as Dewey, trained in the Civil War blockade of the South, interpreted them, the German officers were actively familiar both with the Spanish officials of Manila and with the insurgents. Finally they ensconced themselves in the quarantine station at the entrance of the Bay, and Admiral Diedrichs took up land quarters. Further, they interfered between the insurgents and the Spaniards outside of Manila Bay. In the controversy between Diedrichs and Dewey which grew out of these difficulties, Captain Chichester, commanding the British squadron, supported Dewey's course unqualifiedly and, moreover, let it be clearly known that, in the event of hostilities, the British vessels would take their stand with the Americans.

# CHAPTER IX

### THE BLOCKADE OF CUBA

WHILE the first victory of the war was in the Far East and the possibility of events of world-wide significance hung upon the level-headedness of Commodore Dewey at Manila, it was realized that the war must really be fought in the West. Both President McKinley and the Queen Regent of Spain had issued proclamations stating that they would adhere to the rules of the Declaration of Paris and not resort to the use of privateers. The naval contest, therefore, was confined to the regular navies. Actually the American fleet was superior in battleships, monitors, and protected cruisers; the Spanish was the better equipped in armored cruisers, gunboats, and destroyers.

Both Spain and the United States hastily purchased, in the last days of peace, a few vessels, but not enough seriously to affect their relative strength. Both also drew upon their own merchant marines. Spain added 18 medium-sized vessels to her navy; the United States added in all 123, most of which were small and used for scouting purposes. The largest and most efficient of these additional American ships were the subsidized *St. Paul*, *St. Louis*, *New York*, and *Paris* of the American line, of which the last two, renamed the *Harvard* and *Yale*, proved to be of great service. It was characteristic of American conditions that 28 were private yachts, of which the *Mayflower* was the most notable. To man these new ships, the personnel of the American Navy was increased from 13,750 to 24,123, of whom a large number were men who had received some training in the naval reserves of the various States.

The first duty of the navy was to protect the American coast. In 1885 the War Department had planned and Congress had sanctioned a system of coast defense. Up to 1898, however, only one quarter of the sum considered necessary had been appropriated. Mines and torpedoes were laid at the entrances to American harbors as soon as war broke out, but there was a lack of high-power guns. Rumors of a projected raid by the fast Spanish armored cruisers kept the coast cities in a state of high excitement, and many sought, by petition and political pressure, to compel the Navy Department to detach vessels for their defense. The Naval War Board, however, had to remember that it must protect not only the coast but commerce also, and that the United States was at war not to defend herself but to attack. Cuba was the objective; and Cuba must be cut off from Spain by blockade, and the seas must be made safe for the passage of the American Army. If the navy were to accomplish all these purposes, it must destroy the Spanish Navy. To achieve this end, it would have to work upon the principle of concentration and not dispersion.

For several months before the actual declaration of war with Spain, the Navy Department had been effecting this concentration. On the 21st of April, Captain William T. Sampson was appointed to command the forces on the North Atlantic station. This included practically the whole fleet, except the Pacific squadron under Dewey, and the *Oregon*, a new battleship of unusual design, which was on the Pacific coast. On the 1st of March she was ordered from the Bremerton Yard, in the State of Washington, to San Francisco, and thence to report in the Atlantic. Her voyage was the longest emergency run undertaken up to that time by a

modern battleship.    The outbreak of the war with
Spain meant the sealing of all ports in which she
might have been repaired in case of emergency.
Rumors were rife of Spanish vessels ready to inter-
cept her, and the eyes not only of the United States
but of the world were upon the *Oregon*.   A feeling
of relief and rejoicing therefore passed through the
country when this American warship arrived at
Key West on the 26th of May, fit for immediate
and efficient service.

The fleet, though concentrated in the Atlantic
within the region of immediate hostility, was divided for purposes of operation into a major division under the immediate command of Admiral
Sampson and a flying squadron under Commodore
Schley.[1]   The first undertook the enforcement of
the blockade which was declared on the 21st of
April against Cuba, and patrolled the northern
coast from Gardenas to Bahia.   Key West was
soon filled with Spanish prizes.   On the 27th of
April a brush took place between batteries at Ma-
tanzas and some of the American vessels, without

[1] A patrol squadron of cruisers under Commodore Howell was also
established to protect the coast from the Delaware capes to eastern
Maine.   "It can scarcely be supposed," writes Admiral Chadwick,
"that such action was taken but in deference to the unreasoning fear
of dwellers on the coast."

loss of life on either side, except for a mule which bids fair to become immortal in history through being reported by the Spanish as their only casualty and the first of the war. Admiral Sampson, following the tradition of the American Navy of aiming at a vital spot, wished to attack Havana; and a careful study of its fortifications seems to show that he would have had a good chance of success. Chance, however, might have caused the loss of some of his vessels, and, with the small margin of naval superiority at its disposal the Naval War Board was probably wise in not allowing him to take the risk.

It was, in fact, Spain which took the initiative and decided the matter. Her West India Squadron was weak, even on paper, and was in a condition which would have made it madness to attempt to meet the Americans without reënforcement. She therefore decided to dispatch a fighting fleet from her home forces. Accordingly on the 29th of April, Admiral Cervera left the Cape Verde Islands and sailed westward with one fast second-class battleship, the *Cristóbal Colón*, three armored cruisers, and two torpedo-boat destroyers. It was a reasonably powerful fleet as fleets went in the Spanish War, yet it is difficult to see just what good it could accomplish when it arrived on the scene of action. The naval superiority in the West Indies would still be in the hands of the concentrated American Navy, for the Spanish forces would still be divided, only more equally, between Spanish and Caribbean waters. The American vessels, moreover, would be within easy distance of their home stations, which could supply them with every necessity. The islands belonging to Spain, on the other hand, were ill equipped to become the base of naval operations. Admiral Cervera realized to the full the difficulty of the situation and protested against an expedition which he feared would mean the fall of Spanish power, but public opinion forced the ministry, and he was obliged to put to sea.

For nearly a month the Spanish fleet was lost to sight, and dwellers on the American coast were in a panic of apprehension. Cervera's objective was guessed to be everything from a raid on Bar Harbor to an attack on the *Oregon*, then on its shrouded voyage from the Pacific coast. Cities on the Atlantic seaboard clamored for protection, and the Spanish fleet was magnified by the mist of uncertainty until it became a national terror. Sampson, rightly divining that Cervera would make for

San Juan, the capital and chief seaport of Porto Rico, detached from his blockading force a fighting squadron with which he sailed east, but not finding the Spanish fleet he turned back to Key West. Schley, with the Flying Squadron, was then ordered to Cienfuegos. In the meantime Cervera was escaping detection by the American scouts by taking an extremely southerly course; and with the information that Sampson was off San Juan, the Spanish Admiral sailed for Santiago de Cuba, where he arrived on May 19, 1898.

Though Cervera was safe in harbor, the maneuver of the American fleet cannot be called unsuccessful. Cervera would have preferred to be at San Juan, where there was a navy yard and where his position would have obliged the American fleet either to split into two divisions separated by eight hundred miles or to leave him free range of action. Next to San Juan he would have preferred Havana or Cienfuegos, which were connected by railroad and near which lay the bulk of the Spanish Army. He found himself instead at the extreme eastern end of Cuba in a port with no railroad connection with Havana, partly blocked by the insurgents, and totally unable to supply him with necessities.

Unless Cervera could leave Santiago, his expedition would obviously have been useless. Though it was the natural function of the American fleet to blockade him, for a week after his arrival there was an interesting game of hide and seek between the two fleets. The harbors of Cienfuegos and of Santiago are both landlocked by high hills, and Cervera had entered Santiago without being noticed by the Americans, as that part of the coast was not under blockade. Schley thought Cervera was at Cienfuegos; Sampson was of the opinion that he was at Santiago. When it became known that the enemy had taken refuge in Santiago, Schley began the blockade on the 28th of May, but stated that he could not continue long in position owing to lack of coal. On the 1st of June Sampson arrived and assumed command of the blockading squadron.

With the bottling up of Cervera, the first stage of the war passed. The navy had performed its primary function: it had established its superiority and had obtained the control of the seas. The American coast was safe; American commerce was safe except in the vicinity of Spain; and the sea was open for the passage of an American expeditionary force. Nearly the whole island of Cuba was now under blockade, and the insurgents were receiving supplies from the United States. It had been proved that the fairly even balance of the two fleets, so anxiously scanned when it was reported in the newspapers in April, was entirely deceptive when it came to real efficiency in action. Moreover, the skillful handling of the fleets by the Naval War Board as well as by the immediate commanders had redoubled the actual superiority of the American naval forces.

A fleet in being, even though inferior and immobilized, still counts as a factor in naval warfare, and Cervera, though immobilized by Sampson, himself immobilized the greater number of American vessels necessary to blockade him. The importance of this fact was evident to every one when, in the middle of June, the remainder of the Spanish home fleet, whipped hastily into a semblance of fighting condition, set out eastward under Admiral Camara to contest the Philippines with Dewey. It was impossible for the United States to detach a force sufficient to cross the Atlantic and, without a base, meet this fleet in its home waters. Even if a smaller squadron were dispatched from the Atlantic round Cape Horn, it would arrive in the Philippines too late to be of assistance to Dewey. The two monitors on the Pacific coast, the *Monterey* and the *Monadnock*, had already been ordered across the Pacific, a voyage perilous for vessels of their structure and agonizing to their crews; but it was doubtful whether they or Camara would arrive first in the Philippines.

The logic of the situation demanded that the main American fleet be released. Cervera must be destroyed or held in some other way than at the expense of inactivity on the part of the American warships. Santiago could not be forced by the navy. Two methods remained. The first and simpler expedient was to make the harbor mouth impassable and in this way to bottle up the Spanish fleet. It was decided to sink the collier *Merrimac* at a narrow point in the channel, where, lying full length, she would completely prevent egress. It was a delicate task and one of extraordinary danger. It was characteristic of the spirit of the fleet that, as Admiral Chadwick says, practically all the men were volunteers. The honor of the command was given to Lieutenant Richmond Pearson Hobson, Assistant Naval Constructor, who had been in charge of the preparations. With a crew of six men he entered the harbor mouth on the night of the 3d of June. A shell disabled the steering gear of the *Merrimac*, and the ship sank too far within the harbor to block the entrance entirely. Admiral Cervera himself rescued the crew, assured Sampson of their safety in an appreciative note; and one of the best designed and most heroic episodes in our history just missed success.

The failure of the *Merrimac* experiment left the situation as it had been and forced the American command to consider the second method which would release the American fleet. This new plan contemplated the reduction of Santiago by a combined military and naval attack. Cervera's choice of Santiago therefore practically determined the direction of the first American overseas military expedition, which had been in preparation since the war began.

# CHAPTER X

## THE PREPARATION OF THE ARMY

WHEN one compares the conditions under which the Spanish American War was fought with those of the Great War, he feels himself living in a different age. Twenty years ago hysteria and sudden panics swept the nation. Cheers and waving handkerchiefs and laughing girls sped the troops on their way. It cannot be denied that the most popular song of the war time was *There'll be a hot time in the old town to-night*, though it may be believed that the energy and swing of the music rather than the words made it so. The atmosphere of the country was one of a great national picnic where each one was expected to carry his own lunch. There was apparent none of the concentration of effort and of the calm foresight so necessary for efficiency in modern warfare. For youth the Spanish American War was a great adventure; for the nation it was a diversion sanctioned by a high purpose.

This abandon was doubtless in part due to a comfortable consciousness of the vast disparity in resources between Spain and the United States, which, it was supposed, meant automatically a corresponding difference in fighting strength. The United States did, indeed, have vast superiorities which rendered unnecessary any worry over many of the essentials which gripped the popular mind during the Great War. People believed that the country could supply the munitions needed, and that of facilities for transport it had enough. If the United States did not have at hand exactly the munitions needed, if the transportation system had not been built to launch an army into Cuba, it was popularly supposed that the wealth of the country rendered such trifles negligible, and that, if insufficient attention had been given to the study of such matters in the past, American ingenuity would quickly offset the lack of skilled military experience. The fact that American soldiers traveled in sleeping cars while European armies were transported in freight cars blinded Americans for a while to the significant fact that there was but a single track leading to Tampa, the principal point of embarkation for Cuba; and no one thought of building another.

Nothing so strongly marks the amateur character of the conduct of the Spanish War as the activity of the American press. The navy was dogged by press dispatch boats which revealed its every move. When Admiral Sampson started upon his cruise to San Juan, he requested the press boats to observe secrecy, and Admiral Chadwick comments with satisfaction upon the fact that this request was observed "fully and honorably . . . by every person except one." When Lieutenant Whitney risked his life as a spy in order to investigate conditions in Porto Rico, his plans and purpose were blazoned in the press. Incredible as it may now seem, the newspaper men appear to have felt themselves part of the army. They offered their services as equals, and William Randolph Hearst even ordered one of his staff to sink a vessel in the Suez Canal to delay Camara on his expedition against Dewey. This order, fortunately for the international reputation of the United States, was not executed. With all their blare and childish enthusiasm, the reporters do not seem to have been so successful in revealing to Americans the plans of Spain as they were in furnishing her with itemized accounts of all the doings of the American forces.

While the press not only revealed but formulated

courses of action in the case of the army, the navy, at least, was able to follow its own plans. For this difference there were several causes, chief of which was the fact that the navy was a fully professional arm, ready for action both in equipment and in plans, and able to take a prompt initiative in carrying out an aggressive campaign. The War Department had a more difficult task in adjusting itself to the new conditions brought about by the Spanish American War. The army was made up on the principle traditionally held in the United States that the available army force in time of peace should be just sufficient for the purposes of peace, and that it should be enlarged in time of war. To allow a fair amount of expansion without too much disturbance to the organization in increasing to war strength, the regular army was overofficered in peace times. The chief reliance in war was placed upon the militia. The organization and training of this force was left, however, under a few very general directions, to the various States. As a result, its quality varied and it was nowhere highly efficient in the military sense. Some regiments, it is true, were impressive on parade, but almost none of the officers knew anything of actual modern warfare. There had been no preliminary sifting of ability in the army, and it was only as experience gave the test that the capable and informed were called into positions of importance. In fact, the training of the regular officers was inferior to that of the naval officers. West Point and Annapolis were both excellent in the quality of their instruction, but what they offered amounted only to a college course, and in the army there was no provision for systematic graduate study corresponding to the Naval War College at Newport.

These difficulties and deficiencies, however, cannot fully explain the woeful inferiority of the army to the navy in preparedness. Fundamentally the defect was at the top. Russell A. Alger, the Secretary of War, was a veteran of the Civil War and a silver-voiced orator, but his book on the *Spanish-American War*, which was intended as a vindication of his record, proves that even eighteen months of as grueling denunciation as any American official has ever received could not enlighten him as to what were the functions of his office. Nor did he correct or supplement his own incompetence by seeking professional advice. There existed no general staff, and it did not occur to him, as it did to Secretary Long, to create one to advise him unofficially. He was on bad terms with Major General Nelson A. Miles, who was the general in command. He discussed even the details of questions of army strategy, not only with Miles but with the President and members of the Cabinet. One of the most extraordinary decisions made during his tenure of office was that the act of the 9th of March, appropriating $50,000,000 "for national defense," forbade money to be spent or even contracts to be made by the quartermaster, the commissary, or the surgeon general. In his book Secretary Alger records with pride the fact that all this money was spent for coast defense. In view of the fact that the navy did its task, this expenditure was absolutely unnecessary and served merely to solace coast cities and munition makers.

The regular army on April 1, 1898, consisted of 28,183 officers and men. An act of the 26th of April authorized its increase to about double that size. As enlistment was fairly prompt, by August the army consisted of 56,365 officers and men, the number of officers being but slightly increased. It was decided not to use the militia as it was then organized, but to rely for numbers as usual chiefly upon a volunteer army, authorized by the Act of the 22d of April, and by subsequent acts raised to a total of 200,000, with an additional 3000 cavalry,

3500 engineers, and 10,000 "immunes," or men supposed not to be liable to tropical diseases. The war seemed equally popular all over the country, and the million who offered themselves for service were sufficient to allow due consideration for equitable state quotas and for physical fitness. There were also sufficient Krag-Jörgensen rifles to arm the increased regular army and Springfields for the volunteers.

To provide an adequate number of officers for the volunteer army was more difficult. Even though a considerable number were transferred from the regular to the volunteer army, they constituted only a small proportion of the whole number necessary. Some few of those appointed were graduates of West Point, and more had been in the militia. The great majority, however, had purely amateur experience, and many not even so much. Those who did know something, moreover, did not have the same knowledge or experience. This raw material was given no officer training whatsoever but was turned directly to the task of training the rank and file. Nor were the appointments of new officers confined to the lower ranks. The country, still mindful of its earlier wars, was charmed with the sentimental elevation of confederate generals to the rank of major general in the new army, though a public better informed would hardly have welcomed for service in the tropics the selection of men old enough to be generals in 1865 and then for thirty-three years without military experience in an age of great development in the methods of warfare. The other commanding officers were as old and were mostly chosen by seniority in a service retiring at sixty-four. The unwonted strain of active service naturally proved too great. At the most critical moment of the campaign in Cuba, the commanding general, William R. Shafter, had eaten nothing for four days, and his plucky second in command, the wiry Georgian cavalry leader of 1864 and 1865, General "Joe" Wheeler, was not physically fit to succeed him. There is not the least doubt that the fighting spirit of the men was strong and did not fail, but the defect in those branches of knowledge which are required to keep an army fit to fight is equally certain. The primary cause for the melting of the American army by disease must be acknowledged to be the insufficient training of the officers.

This hit or miss method, however, had its compensations, for it brought about some appointments of unusual merit. Conspicuous were those of Colonel Leonard Wood and Lieutenant Colonel

Theodore Roosevelt. The latter had resigned as Assistant Secretary of the Navy, a position in which he had contributed a great deal to the efficiency of that Department, in order to take a more tangible part in the war. After raising among his friends and the cowboys of the West a regiment of "Rough Riders," he declined its command on plea of military inexperience. Roosevelt made one of those happy choices which are a mark of his administrative ability in selecting as colonel Leonard Wood, an army surgeon whose quality he knew through common experiences in the West.

To send into a midsummer tropical jungle an American army, untrained to take care of its health, for the most part clothed in the regulation army woolens, and tumbled together in two months, was an undertaking which could be justified only on the ground that the national safety demanded immediate action. In 1898, however, it seemed to be universally taken for granted by people and administration, by professional soldier as well as by public sentiment, that the army must invade Cuba without regard to its fitness for such active service. The responsibility for this decision must rest upon the nation. The experience of centuries had proved conspicuously that climate was the strongest defense of the Caribbean islands against invasion, and it was in large measure the very sacrifice of so many American soldiers that induced the study of tropical diseases. In 1898 it could hardly be expected that the American command, inexperienced and eager for action, should have recognized the mosquito as the carrier of yellow fever and the real enemy, or should have realized the necessity of protecting the soldiers by inoculation against typhoid fever.

Fixed as was the determination to send an army into Cuba at the earliest possible moment, there had been a wide diversity of opinion as to what should be the particular objective. General Miles wavered between the choice of the island of Porto Rico and Puerto Principe, a city in the interior and somewhat east of the middle of Cuba; the Department hesitated between Tunás on the south coast of Cuba, within touch of the insurgents, and Mariel on the north, the seizure of which would be the first step in a siege of Havana. The situation at Santiago, however, made that city the logical objective of the troops, and on the 31st of May, General Shafter was ordered to be prepared to move. On the 7th of June he was ordered to sail with "not less than 10,000 men," but an alarming, though unfounded, rumor of a Spanish squadron off the north coast of Cuba delayed the expedition until the 14th. With an army of seventeen thousand on thirty-two transports, and accompanied by eighty-nine newspaper correspondents, Shafter arrived on the 20th of June off Santiago.

The Spanish troops in Cuba — the American control of the sea made it unnecessary to consider those available in Spain — amounted, according to returns in April, 1898, to 196,820. This formidable number, however, was not available at any one strategic spot owing to the difficulty of transporting either troops or supplies, particularly at the eastern end of the island, in the neighborhood of Santiago. It was estimated that the number of men of use about Santiago was about 12,000, with 5000 approaching to assist. Perhaps 3000 insurgents were at hand under General Garcia. The number sent, then, was not inadequate to the task. Equal numbers are not, indeed, ordinarily considered sufficient for an offensive campaign against fortifications, but the American commanders counted upon a difference in morale between the two armies, which was justified by results. Besides the American Army could be reinforced as necessity arose.

# CHAPTER XI

## THE CAMPAIGN OF SANTIAGO DE CUBA

IN planning the campaign against Santiago, Admiral Sampson wished the army immediately to assault the defenses at the harbor mouth in order to open the way for the navy. General Shafter, however, after conferring with General Garcia, the commander of the insurgents, decided to march overland against the city. The army did not have sufficient small vessels to effect a landing; but the navy came to its assistance, and on the 22d of June the first American troops began to disembark at Daiquiri, though it was not until the 26th that the entire expedition was on shore. On the second day Siboney, which had a better anchorage and was some six miles closer to Santiago, was made the base. From Siboney there stretched for eight or ten miles a rolling country covered with heavy jungle brush and crossed by mere threads of roads. There was indeed a railroad, but this followed a roundabout route by the coast. Through this novel and extremely uncomfortable country, infected with mosquitoes, the troops pressed, eager to meet the enemy.

The first engagement took place at Las Guasimas, on the 24th of June. Here a force of about a thousand dismounted cavalry, partly regulars and partly Rough Riders, defeated nearly twice their number of Spaniards. This was the only serious resistance which the Americans encountered until they reached the advanced defenses of Santiago. The next week they spent in getting supplies ashore, improving the roads, and reconnoitering. The newspapers considered this interval entirely too long! The 30th of June found the Americans confronting the main body of Spaniards in position, and on the 1st of July, the two armies joined battle.

Between the opposing forces was the little river San Juan and its tributaries. The Spanish left wing was at El Caney, supported by a stone blockhouse, rifle pits, and barbed wire, but with no artillery. About four miles away was San Juan Hill, with more formidable works straddling the main road which led to Santiago. Opposite El Caney, General Lawton was in command of about seven thousand Americans. The fight here began at half-past six in the morning, but the American artillery was placed at too great a distance to be very effective. The result was a long and galling exchange of rifle firing, which is apt to prove trying to raw troops. The infantry, however, advanced with persistency and showed marked personal initiative as they pushed forward under such protection as the brush and grass afforded until they finally rushed a position which gave opportunity to the artillery. After this they speedily captured the blockhouse.

The fight lasted over eight hours instead of two, as had been expected, and thus delayed General Lawton, who was looked for at San Juan by the American left. The losses, too, were heavy, the total casualties amounting to seven per cent of the force engaged. The Americans, however, had gained the position, and after a battle which had been long and serious enough to test thoroughly the quality of the personnel of the army. Whatever deficiencies the Americans may have had in organization, training, and military education, they undoubtedly possessed fighting spirit, courage, and personal ingenuity, and these are, after all, the qualities for which builders of armies look.

The battle of El Caney was perhaps unnecessary, for the position lay outside the main Spanish line and would probably have been abandoned when San Juan fell. For that more critical movement General Shafter kept about eight thousand troops and the personal command. Both he and General Wheeler, however, were suffering from the climate and were unable to be with the troops. The problem of making a concerted advance through the thick underbrush was a difficult one, and the disposition of the American troops was at once revealed by a battery of artillery which used black powder, and by a captive balloon which was injudiciously towed about.

The right wing here, after assuming an exposed position, was unable to act, as Lawton, by whom it was expecting to be reinforced, was delayed at El Caney. The advance regiments were under the fire of the artillery, the infantry, and the skillful sharpshooters of an invisible enemy and were also exposed to the fierce heat of the sun, to which they were unaccustomed. The wounded were carried back on litters, turned over to the surgeons, who worked manfully with the scantiest of equipment, and were then laid, often naked except for their bandages, upon the damp ground. Regiment blocked regiment in the narrow road, and officers carrying orders were again and again struck, as they emerged from cover, by the sharpshooters' fire. The want of means of communication paralyzed the command, for all the equipment of a modern army was lacking: there were no aeroplanes, no wireless stations, no telephones.

Throughout the morning the situation grew worse, but the nerve of the men did not give way, and American individual initiative rose to the boiling point. Realizing that safety lay only in advance, the officers on the spot began to take control. General Hawkins, with the Sixth and Sixteenth Regulars, advanced against the main blockhouse, which crested a slope of two hundred feet, and the men of the Seventy-first New York Volunteers joined promiscuously in the charge.

To the right rose Kettle Hill, jutting out and flanking the approach to the main position. Facing it and dismounted were the First and Ninth Regular Cavalry, the latter a negro regiment, and the Rough Riders under Colonel Roosevelt. The Tenth Infantry was between the two wings, and divided in the support of both. A battery of Gatling guns was placed in position. The Americans steadily advanced in an irregular line, though kept in some sort of formation by their officers. Breaking down brush and barbed wire and sheltering themselves in the high grass, the men on the right wing worked their way up Kettle Hill, but before they reached the rifle pits of the enemy, they saw the Spaniards retreating on the run. The audacity of the Americans at the critical moment had insured the ultimate success of their attack and they found the final capture of the hill easy.

The longer charge against the center of the enemy was in the meantime being pressed home, under the gallant leadership of General Hawkins, who at times was far in advance of his line. The men of the right wing who looked down from their new position on Kettle Hill, a quarter of a mile distant, saw the Spaniards give way and the American center dash forward. In order to support this advance movement, the Gatlings were brought to Kettle Hill, and General S. S. Sumner and Colonel Roosevelt led their men down Kettle and up San Juan Hill, where they swept over the northern jut only a moment after Hawkins had carried the main blockhouse.

The San Juan position now in the hands of the Americans was the key of Santiago, but that intrenched city lay a mile and a quarter distant and had still to be unlocked — a task which presented no little difficulty. The Americans, it is true, had an advantageous position on a hilltop, but the enemy had retired only a quarter of a mile and were supported by the complete system of fortifications which protected Santiago. The American losses totaled fifteen hundred, a number just about made good at this moment by the arrival of General Duffield's brigade, which had followed the main expedition. The number of the Spanish force, which was unknown to the Americans, was increased on the 3d of July by the arrival of a relief expedition under Colonel Escario, with about four thousand men whom the insurgent forces had failed to meet and block, as had been planned.

On the 2d of July there was desultory fighting, and on the 3d, General Shafter telegraphed to the Secretary of War that he was considering the withdrawal of his troops to a strong position, about five miles in the rear. The Secretary immediately replied: "Of course you can judge the situation better than we can at this end of the line. If, however, you could hold your present position, especially San Juan Heights, the effect upon the country would be much better than falling back."

The Spanish commanders, however, did not share General Shafter's view as to the danger involving the Americans. Both Admiral Cervera and General Blanco considered that the joint operations of the American Army and Navy had rendered the reduction of Santiago only a question of time, but they differed as to the course to be pursued. In the end, General Blanco, who was in supreme command, decided, after an exchange of views with the Spanish Government and a consultation with the Captain of the German cruiser *Geier*, then at Havana, to order the Spanish squadron to attempt an escape from Santiago harbor. Cervera's sailors had hitherto been employed in the defense of the city, but with the arrival of the reinforcements under Escario he found it possible to reman his fleet. An attempt to escape in the dark seemed impossible because of the unremitting glare of the searchlights of the American vessels. Cervera determined upon the desperate expedient of steaming out in broad daylight and making for Cienfuegos.

The blockade systematically planned by Admiral Sampson was conducted with a high degree of efficiency. Each American ship had its definite place and its particular duty. When vessels were obliged to coal at Guantánamo, forty miles distant, the next in line covered the cruising interval. The American combined squadron was about double

Cervera's in strength; his ships, however, were supposed to have the advantage in speed, and it was conceivable that, by turning sharply to the one side or the other, they might elude the blockading force. On the very day that Cervera made his desperate dash out of the harbor, as it happened, the *New York*, Admiral Sampson's flagship, was out of line, taking the Admiral to a conference with General Shafter at Siboney, a few miles to the eastward. The absence of the flagship, however, in no way weakened the blockade, for, if Cervera turned westward he would find the squadron of Schley and the other vessels designated to prevent his escape in that direction, while if he turned eastward he would almost at once be engaged with the *New York*, which would then be in an advantageous position ahead of the chase.

At half-past nine on the morning of the 3d of July, the first vessel of the Spanish fleet emerged from Santiago Harbor. By 10:10 A.M. all the Spanish ships were outside of the harbor mouth. Commodore Schley, on the *Brooklyn*, hoisted the signal to "close up," apparently on the understanding that Sampson's signal on leaving for Siboney to "Disregard motions of the commander-in-chief" had delegated the command to him.

Though this question of command later involved a bitter dispute, it was at the time of little moment, for clouds of smoke obscured the signals so frequently that no complicated maneuver could have been guided by them, and, as far as concerted action was concerned, the whole squadron was under exactly similar contingent orders from Admiral Sampson. As a matter of fact, the thing to do was so obvious that the subsequent dispute really raged on the point of who actually gave an order, the sense of which every one of the commanders would have executed without order. If, therefore, the layman feels some annoyance at such a controversy over naval red tape, he may have the consolation of knowing that all concerned, admirals and captains, did the right and sensible thing at the time. If there be an exception, it was the curious maneuver of Schley, the commander of the *Brooklyn*, who turned a complete circle away from the enemy after the battle had begun. This action of his was certainly not due to a desire to escape, for the *Brooklyn* quickly turned again into the fight. A controversy, too, has raged over this maneuver. Was it undertaken because the *Brooklyn* was about to be rammed by the *Vizcaya*, or because Schley thought that his position blocked the fire of the other American vessels? It is not unlikely that the commander of the Spanish ship hoped to ram the *Brooklyn*, which was, because of her speed, a most redoubtable foe. But unless this maneuver saved the *Brooklyn*, it had little result except to scare the *Texas*, upon whom she suddenly bore down out of a dense cloud of smoke.

Steering westward, the Spanish ships attempted to pass the battle line, but the American vessels kept pace with them. For a short time the engagement was very severe, for practically all vessels of both fleets took part, and the Spanish harbor batteries added their fire. At 10:15 A.M. the *Maria Teresa*, Admiral Cervera's flagship, on fire and badly shattered by heavy shells, turned toward the beach. Five minutes later the *Oquendo*, after something of a duel with the *Texas*, also turned inshore. The *Brooklyn* was in the lead of the Americans, closely followed by the *Oregon*, which developed a wonderful burst of speed in excess of that called for in her contract. These two ships kept up the chase of the *Vizcaya* and the *Cristóbal Colón*, while the slower vessels of the fleet attended to the two Spanish destroyers, *Furor* and *Pluton*. At 11:15 A.M. the *Vizcaya*, riddled by fire from the *Brooklyn* and *Oregon*, gave up the fight.

By this time, Sampson in the *New York* was rapidly approaching the fight, and now ordered the majority of the vessels back to their stations. The *Colón*, fleeing westward and far ahead of the American ships, was pursued by the *Brooklyn*, the *Oregon*, the *Texas*, the *New York*, and the armed yacht *Vixen*. It was a stern chase, although the American vessels had some advantage by cutting across a slight concave indentation of the coast, while the *Colón* steamed close inshore. At 1:15 P.M. a shot from the *Oregon* struck ahead of the *Colón*, and it was evident that she was covered by the American guns. At 1:30 P.M. she gave over her flight and made for shore some forty-five miles west of Santiago. The victory was won. It has often been the good fortune of Americans to secure their greatest victories on patriotic anniversaries and thereby to enhance the psychological effect. Admiral Sampson was able to announce to the American people, as a Fourth of July present, the destruction of the Spanish fleet with the loss of but one of his men and but slight damage to his ships.

On the hills above Santiago the American Army had now only the land forces of the Spaniards to contend with. Shafter's demand for unconditional surrender met with a refusal, and there ensued a week of military quiet. During this time General Shafter conducted a correspondence with the War Department, in judging which it is charitable to remember that the American commander weighed three hundred pounds, that he was sweltering under a hot sun, and that he was sixty-three years old, and sick. Too humane to bombard Santiago while Hobson and his men were still in Spanish hands, he could not forgive Sampson for not having forced the narrow and well-mined channel at the risk of his fleet. The War Department, sharing Shafter's indignation, prepared to attempt the entrance with one of its own transports protected by baled hay, as had been done on the Mississippi during the Civil War. Shafter continued to be alarmed at the situation. Without reënforcements he could not attack, and he proposed to allow the Spaniards to evacuate. The War Department forbade this alternative and, on the 10th of July, he began the bombardment of Santiago.

The Secretary of War then hit upon the really happy though quite unmilitary device of offering, in return for unconditional surrender, to transport the Spanish troops, at once and without parole, back to their own country. Secretary Alger was no unskillful politician, and he was right in believing that this device, though unconventional, would make a strong appeal to an army three years away from home and with dwindling hopes of ever seeing Spain again. On the 15th of July a capitulation was agreed upon, and the terms of surrender included not only the troops in Santiago but all those in that military district — about twenty-four thousand men, with cannon, rifles, ammunition, rations, and other military supplies. Shafter's recommendation that the troops be allowed to carry their arms back to Spain with them was properly refused by the War Department. Arrangements were made for Spanish ships paid by the United States to take the men immediately to Spain. This extraordinary operation was begun on the 8th of August, while the war was still in progress, and was accomplished before peace was established.

The Santiago campaign, like the Mexican War, was fought chiefly by regulars. The Rough Riders and the Seventy-first New York Regiment were the only volunteer units to take a heavy share. Yet the absence of effective staff management was so marked that, as compared with the professional accuracy shown by the navy, the whole campaign on land appears as an amateur undertaking. But the individual character of both volunteers and regulars was high. The American victory was fundamentally due to the fighting spirit of the men and to the individual initiative of the line and field officers.

In the meantime the health of the American Army was causing grave concern to its more observant leaders. Six weeks of Cuban climate had taken out of the army all that exuberant energy which it had brought with it from the north. The army had accomplished its purpose only at the complete sacrifice of its fighting strength. Had the Spanish commander possessed more nerve and held out a little longer, he might well have seen his victorious enemies wither before his eyes, as the British had before Cartagena in 1741. On the 3d of August a large number of the officers of the Santiago army, including Generals Wheeler, Sumner, and Lawton, and Colonel Roosevelt, addressed a round robin to General Shafter on the alarming condition of the army. Its substance is indicated in the following sentences: "This army must be moved at once or it will perish. As an army it can be safely moved now. Persons responsible for preventing such a move will be responsible for the unnecessary loss of many thousands of lives." Already on the 1st of August, General Shafter had reported 4255 sick, of whom 3164 were cases of yellow fever, that deadly curse of Cuba, which the lack of proper quarantine had so often allowed to invade the shores of the United States. On the 3d of August, even before General Shafter had received the round robin, the Secretary of War authorized the withdrawal of at least a portion of the army, which was to be replaced by supposedly immune regiments. By the middle of August, the soldiers began to arrive at Camp Wikoff at Montauk Point, on the eastern end of Long Island. Through this camp, which had been hastily put into condition to receive them, there passed about thirty-five thousand soldiers, of whom twenty thousand were sick. When the public saw those who a few weeks before had been healthy and rollicking American boys, now mere skeletons, borne helpless in stretchers and looking old and shriveled, a wave of righteous indignation against Secretary Alger swept over the country, and eventually accomplished enough to prevent such catastrophes in the future.

The distressing experience of the army was too real not to have its constructive effect. Men like William Crawford Gorgas were inspired to study the sanitation and the diseases of the tropics and have now made it possible for white men to live there safely. Men of affairs like Elihu Root were stimulated to give their talents to army administration. Fortunately the boys were brought north just in time to save their lives, and the majority, after a recuperation of two or three years, regained their normal health.

The primary responsibility for this gamble with death rested with those who sent an expedition from the United States to the tropics in midsummer when the measures necessary to safeguard its health were not yet known. This responsibility rested immediately upon the American people themselves, all too eager for a war for which they were not prepared and for a speedy victory at all costs. For this national impatience they had to pay dearly. The striking contrast, however, between the efficiency of the navy and the lack of preparation on the part of the army shows that the people as a whole would have supported a more thorough preparation of the army, had the responsible officials possessed sufficient courage and intelligence to have demanded it; nor would the people have been unwilling to defer victory until autumn, had they been honestly informed of the danger of tropical disease into which they were sending the flower of their youth. Such a postponement would not only have meant better weather but it would have given time to teach the new officers their duty in safeguarding the health of their men as far as possible, and this precaution alone would have saved many lives. Owing to the greater practical experience of the officers in the regular regiments, the death rate among the men in their ranks fell far below that among the volunteers, even though many of the men with the regulars had enlisted after the declaration of war. On the other hand, speed as well as sanitation was an element in the war, and the soldier who was sacrificed to lack of preparation may be said to have served his country no less than he who died in battle. Strategy and diplomacy in this instance were enormously facilitated by the immediate invasion of Cuba, and perhaps the outcome justified the cost. The question of relative values is a difficult one.

No such equation of values, however, can hold the judgment in suspense in the case of the host of secondary errors that grew out of the indolence of Secretary Alger and his worship of politics. Probably General Miles was mistaken in his charge concerning embalmed beef, and possibly the canned beef was not so bad as it tasted; but there can be no excuse for a Secretary of War who did not consider it his business to investigate the question of proper rations for an army in the tropics simply because Congress had, years before, fixed a ration for use within the United States. There was no excuse for sending many of the men clad in heavy army woolens. There was no excuse for not providing a sufficient number of surgeons and abundant hospital service. There was little excuse for the appointment of General Shafter, which was made in part for political reasons. There was no excuse for keeping at the head of the army administration General Nelson A. Miles, with whom, whatever his abilities, the Secretary of War was unable to work.

The navy did not escape controversy. In fact, a war fought under the eyes of hundreds of uncensored newspaper correspondents unskilled in military affairs could not fail to supply a daily grist of scandal to an appreciative public. The controversy between Sampson and Schley, however, grew out of incompatible personalities stirred to rivalry by indiscreet friends and a quarrelsome public. Captain Sampson was chosen to command, and properly so, because of his recognized abilities. Commodore Schley, a genial and open-hearted man, too much given to impulse, though he outranked Sampson, was put under his command. Sampson was not gracious in his treatment of the Commodore, and ill feeling resulted. When the time came to promote both officers for their good conduct, Secretary Long by recommending that Sampson be raised eight numbers and Schley six, reversed their relative positions as they had been before the war. This recommendation, in itself proper, was sustained by the Senate, and all the vitality the controversy ever had then disappeared, though it remains a bone of contention to be gnawed by biographers and historians.

# CHAPTER XII

### THE CLOSE OF THE WAR

WHILE the American people were concentrating their attention upon the blockade of Santiago near their own shores, the situation in the distant islands of the Pacific was rapidly becoming acute. All through June, Dewey had been maintaining himself, with superb nerve, in Manila Harbor, in the midst of uncertain neutrals. A couple of unwieldy United States monitors were moving slowly to his assistance from the one side, while a superior Spanish fleet was approaching from the other. On the 26th of June, the Spanish Admiral Camara had reached Port Said, but he was not entirely happy. Several of his vessels proved to be in that ineffective condition which was characteristic of the Spanish Navy. The Egyptian authorities refused him permission to refit his ships or to coal, and the American consul had with foresight bought up much of the coal which the Spanish

Admiral had hoped to secure and take aboard later from colliers. Nevertheless the fleet passed through the Suez Canal and entered the Red Sea.

Fully alive to the danger of the situation, the Naval War Board gave orders on the 29th of June for a squadron under Commodore Watson to start for the Spanish coast in hope of drawing Camara back.

The alarm which had previously been created on the American coast by the shrouded approach of Cervera naturally suggested that the Americans themselves might win one of those psychological victories now recognized as such an important factor in modern warfare. The chief purpose of future operations was to convince the Spanish people that they were defeated, and nothing would more conduce to this result than to bring war to their doors. This was, moreover, an operation particularly suited to the conditions under which the United States was waging war, for publicity was here a helping factor. Admiral Sampson, more intent on immediate business than on psychological pressure, was not enthusiastically in favor of the plan. Nevertheless preparation proceeded with that deliberation which in this case was part of the game, and presently the shadow of an impending

American attack hung heavy over the coasts of Spain. The Spanish Government at first perhaps considered the order a bluff which the United States would not dare to carry out while Cervera's fleet was so near its own shores; but with the destruction of Cervera's ships the plan became plainly possible, and on the 8th of July the Spanish Government ordered Camara back to parade his vessels before the Spanish cities to assure them of protection.

But, before Camara was called home, the public were watching his advance against the little American fleet at Manila, with an anxiety perhaps greater than Dewey's own. Nothing in modern war equals in dramatic tension the deadly, slow, inevitable approach of a fleet from one side of the world against its enemy on the other. Both beyond the reach of friendly help, each all powerful until it meets its foe, their home countries have to watch the seemingly never coming, but nevertheless certain, clash, which under modern conditions means victory or destruction. It is the highest development of that situation which has been so exploited in a myriad forms by the producers of dramas for the moving pictures and which nightly holds audiences silent; but it plays itself out in war, not in minutes but in months.   No one who lived through that period can ever forget the progress of Camara against Dewey, or that of Rozhestvensky with the Russian fleet, six years later, against Togo.

Meanwhile another move was made in the Caribbean.   General Miles had from the first considered Porto Rico the best immediate objective: it was much nearer Spain than Cuba, was more nearly self-sufficing if left alone, and less defensible if attacked.   The War Department, on the 7th of June, had authorized Miles to assemble thirty thousand troops for the invasion of Porto Rico, and preparations for this expedition were in progress throughout the course of the Santiago campaign.   Miles at the time of the surrender of Santiago was actually off that city with reinforcements, which thereupon at once became available as a nucleus to be used against Porto Rico.   On the 21st of July he left Guantánamo Bay and, taking the Spaniards as well as the War Department completely by surprise as to his point of attack, he effected a landing on the 26th at Guanica, near the southwestern corner of Porto Rico.

The expeditionary force to Porto Rico, however, consisted not of 30,000 men but of only about 15,000; and it was not fully assembled on the island until the 8th of August. The total Spanish forces amounted to only about 10,000, collected on the defensible ground to the north and in the interior, so that they did not disturb the disembarkation. The American Army which had been dispatched from large Atlantic ports, such as Charleston and Newport News, seems to have been better and more systematically equipped than the troops sent to Santiago. The Americans occupied Guanica, Ponce, and Arroyo with little or no opposition, and were soon in possession of the southern shores of the island.

Between the American forces and the main body of the enemy stretched a range of mountains running east and west through the length of the island. San Juan, the only fortress, which was the main objective of the American Army, lay on the opposite side of this mountain range, on the northern coast of the island. The approach to the fortress lay along a road which crossed the hills and which possessed natural advantages for defense. On the 7th of August a forward movement was begun. While General Wilson's army advanced from Ponce along the main road toward San Juan and General Brooke moved north from Arroyo, General Schwan was to clear the western end of the island and work his way

around to Arecibo, toward which General Henry
was to advance through the interior. The American armies systematically worked forward, with an
occasional skirmish in which they were always victorious, and were received with a warm welcome by
the teeming native population. On the 13th of
August, General Wilson was on the point of clearing his first mountain range, General Schwan had
occupied Mayaguez, and General Henry had passed
through the mountains and was marching down
the valley of the Arecibo, when orders arrived from
Washington to suspend operations.

The center of interest, however, remained in the
far-away Philippines. Dewey, who had suddenly
burst upon the American people as their first hero,
remained a fixed star in their admiration, a position in which his own good judgment and the for-
tunate scarcity of newspaper correspondents served
to maintain him. From him action was expected,
and it had been prepared for. Even before news
arrived on the 7th of May of Dewey's victory on
the 1st of May, the Government had anticipated
such a result and had decided to send an army to
support him. San Francisco was made a rendezvous for volunteers, and on the 12th of May, General Wesley Merritt was assigned to command the

expedition. Dewey reported that he could at any time command the surrender of Manila, but that it would be useless unless he had troops to occupy the city.

On the 19th of May, General Merritt received the following orders: "The destruction of the Spanish fleet at Manila, followed by the taking of the naval station at Cavité, the paroling of the garrisons, and the acquisition of the control of the bay, have rendered it necessary, in the further prosecution of the measures adopted by this Government for the purpose of bringing about an honorable and durable peace with Spain, to send an army of occupation to the Philippines for the twofold purpose of completing the reduction of the Spanish power in that quarter and giving order and security to the islands while in the possession of the United States."

On the 30th of June the first military expedition, after a bloodless capture of the island of Guam, arrived in Manila Bay. A second contingent arrived on the 17th of July, and on the 25th, General Merritt himself with a third force, which brought the number of Americans up to somewhat more than 10,000. The Spaniards had about 13,000 men guarding the rather antiquated fortifications of old Manila and a semicircle of blockhouses and trenches thrown about the city, which contained about 350,000 inhabitants.

It would have been easy to compel surrender or evacuation by the guns of the fleet, had it not been for an additional element in the situation. Manila was already besieged, or rather blockaded, on the land side, by an army of nearly ten thousand Philippine insurgents under their shrewd leader, Emilio Aguinaldo. It does not necessarily follow that those who are fighting the same enemy are fighting together, and in this case the relations between the Americans and the insurgents were far from intimate, though Dewey had kept the situation admirably in hand until the arrival of the American troops.

General Merritt decided to hold no direct communication with Aguinaldo until the Americans were in possession of the city, but landed his army to the south of Manila beyond the trenches of the Filipinos. On the 30th of July, General F. V. Greene made an informal arrangement with the Filipino general for the removal of the insurgents from the trenches directly in front of the American forces, and immediately advanced beyond their original position. The situation of Manila was indeed desperate and clearly demanded a surrender to the American forces, who might be relied upon to preserve order and protect property. The Belgian Consul, M. Eduard André, urged this course upon the Spanish commander. The Governor-General, Fermin Jaudenes, exhibited the same spirit which the Spanish commanders revealed throughout the war: though constitutionally indisposed to take any bold action, he nevertheless considered it a point of honor not to recognize the inevitable. He allowed it to be understood that he could not surrender except to an assault, although well knowing that such a *mêlée* might cause the city to be ravaged by the Filipinos. M. André, however, succeeded by the 11th of August in arranging a verbal understanding that the fleet should fire upon the city and that the troops should attack, but that the Spaniards should make no real resistance and should surrender as soon as they considered that their honor was saved.

The chief contestants being thus amicably agreed to a spectacular but bloodless battle, the main interest lay in the future action of the interested and powerful spectators in the harbor. Admiral Dewey, though relieved by the arrival of the monitor *Monterey* on the 4th of August, was by no means certain that the German squadron would stand by without interference and see the city bombarded. On the 9th of August he gave notice of the impending action and ordered foreign vessels out of the range of fire. On the 13th of August Dewey steamed into position before the city. As the American vessels steamed past the British *Immortalité*, her guard paraded and her band played Admiral Dewey's favorite march. Immediately afterwards the British commander, Captain Chichester, moved his vessels toward the city and took a position between our fleet and the German squadron. The foreign vessels made no interference, but the Filipinos were more restless. Eagerly watching the American assault, they rushed forward when they saw it successful, and began firing on the Spaniards just as the latter hoisted the white flag. They were quieted, though with difficulty, and by nightfall the city was under the Stars and Stripes, with American troops occupying the outworks facing the forces of Aguinaldo, who were neither friends nor foes.

While the dispatch of Commodore Watson's fleet to Spain was still being threatened and delayed, while General Miles was rapidly approaching the capital of Porto Rico, and on the same day that Admiral Dewey and General Merritt captured Manila, Spain yielded. On the 18th of July Spain had taken the first step toward peace by asking for the good offices of the French Government. On the 26th of July, M. Cambon, the French Ambassador at Washington, opened negotiations with the United States. On the 12th of August, a protocol was signed, but, owing to the difference in time on the opposite side of the globe, to say nothing of the absence of cable communication, not in time to prevent Dewey's capture of Manila. This protocol provided for the meeting of peace commissioners at Paris not later than the 1st of October. Spain agreed immediately to evacuate and relinquish all claim to Cuba; to cede to the United States ultimately all other islands in the West Indies, and one in the Ladrones; and to permit the United States to "occupy and hold the city, bay, and harbor of Manila pending the conclusion of a treaty of peace which shall determine the control, disposition, and government of the Philippines."

President McKinley appointed the Secretary of State, William R. Day, as president of the peace commission, and summoned John Hay home from England to take his place. The other commissioners were Senators Cushman K. Davis and

William P. Frye, Republicans, Senator George
Gray, Democrat, and Whitelaw Reid, the editor of
the New York *Tribune*. The secretary of the commission was the distinguished student of international law, John Bassett Moore. On most points
there was general agreement as to what they were
to do. Cuba, of course, must be free. It was,
moreover, too obvious to need much argument
that Spanish rule on the American continent must
come altogether to an end. As there was no organized local movement in Porto Rico to take over
the government, its cession to the United States
was universally recognized as inevitable. Nevertheless when the two commissions met in Paris,
there proved to be two exciting subjects of controversy, and at moments it seemed possible that the
attempt to arrange a peace would prove unsuccessful. However reassured the people were by the successful termination of the war, for those in authority
the period of anxiety had not yet entirely passed.

The first of these points was raised by the Spanish commissioners. They maintained that the separation of Cuba from Spain involved the rending of
the Empire, and that Cuba should therefore take
responsibilities as well as freedom. The specific
question was that of debts contracted by Spain, for

the security of which Cuban revenues had been pledged. There was a manifest lack of equity in this claim, for Cuba had not been party to the contracting of the obligations, and the money had been spent in stifling her own desire to be free rather than on the development of her resources. Nevertheless the Spanish commissioners could feel the support of a sustaining public opinion about them, for the bulk of these obligations were held in France and investors were doubtful of the ability of Spain, if bereft of her colonies, to carry her enormous financial burdens. The point, then, was stoutly urged, but the American commissioners as stoutly defended the interests of their clients, the Cubans, and held their ground. Thanks to their efforts, the Cuban republic was born free of debt.

The other point was raised by the American commissioners, and was both more important and more complicated, for when the negotiation began the United States had not fully decided what it wanted. It was necessary first to decide and then to obtain the consent of Spain with regard to the great unsettled question of the disposition of the Philippines. Dewey's victory came as an overwhelming surprise to the great majority of Americans snugly encased, as they supposed themselves to be, in a separate hemisphere. Nearly all looked upon it as a military operation only, not likely to lead to later complications. Many discerning individuals, however, both in this country and abroad, at once saw or feared that occupation would lead to annexation. Carl Schurz, as early as the 9th of May, wrote McKinley expressing the hope that "we remain true to our promise that this is a war of deliverance and not one of greedy ambition, conquest, self-aggrandizement." In August, Andrew Carnegie wrote in *The North American Review* an article on *Distant Possessions—The Parting of the Ways.*

Sentiment in favor of retaining the islands, however, grew rapidly in volume and in strength. John Hay wrote to Andrew Carnegie on the 22d of August: "I am not allowed to say in my present fix (ministerial responsibility) how much I agree with you. The only question in my mind is how far it is now *possible* for us to withdraw from the Philippines. I am rather thankful it is not given to me to solve that momentous question." On the 5th of September, he wrote to John Bigelow: "I fear you are right about the Philippines, and I hope the Lord will be good to us poor devils who have to take care of them. I marvel at your suggesting that we pay for them. I should have expected no less of your probity; but how many except those educated by you in the school of morals and diplomacy would agree with you? Where did I pass you on the road of life? You used to be a little my senior [twenty-one years]; now you are ages younger and stronger than I am. And yet I am going to be Secretary of State for a little while."

Not all those who advocated the retention of the Philippines did so reluctantly or under the pressure of a feeling of necessity. In the very first settlers of our country, the missionary impulse beat strong. John Winthrop was not less intent than Cromwell on the conquest of all humanity by his own ideals; only he believed the most efficacious means to be the power of example instead of force. Just now there was a renewed sense throughout the Anglo-Saxon public that it was the duty of the civilized to promote the civilization of the backward, and the Cromwellian method waxed in popularity. Kipling, at the summit of his influence, appealed to a wide and powerful public in his *White Man's Burden*, which appeared in 1899.

> Take up the White Man's burden —
> Send forth the best ye breed —
> Go bind your sons to exile
> To serve your captives' need;

To wait in heavy harness,
On fluttered folk and wild —
Your new caught, sullen peoples,
Half-devil and half-child.

Take up the White Man's burden —
And reap his old reward:
The blame of those ye better,
The hate of those ye guard —
The cry of hosts ye humour
(Ah, slowly!) towards the light: —
Why brought ye us from bondage,
Our loved Egyptian night?

McKinley asked those having opinions on the subject of this burden to write to him, and a strong call for the United States to take up her share in the regeneration of mankind came from important representatives of the religious public. Nor was the attitude of those different who saw the possibilities of increased traffic with the East. The expansion of the area of home distribution seemed a halfway house between the purely nationalistic policy, which was becoming a little irksome, and the competition of the open world.

It was not, however, the urging of these forces alone which made the undecided feel that the annexation of the Philippines was bound to come. The situation itself seemed to offer no other solution. Gradually evidence as to the local conditions reached America. The Administration was anxious for the commissioners to have the latest information, and, as Admiral Dewey remained indispensable at Manila, General Merritt was ordered to report at Paris, where he arrived on the 6th of October. He was of the opinion that the Americans must remain in the Philippines, and his reports were sustained by a cablegram from Dewey on the 14th of October reading: "Spanish authority has been completely destroyed in Luzon, and general anarchy prevails without the limits of the city and Bay of Manila. Strongly probable that islands to the south will fall into the same state soon." The history of the previous few years and existing conditions made it highly improbable that Spanish domination could ever be restored. The withdrawal of the United States would therefore not mean the reëstablishment of Spanish rule but no government at all.

As to the régime which would result from our withdrawal, Admiral Dewey judged from the condition of those areas where Spanish authority had already ceased and that of the Americans had not yet been established. "Distressing reports," he cabled, "have been received of inhuman cruelty practised on religious and civil authorities in other parts of these islands. The natives appear unable to govern." It was highly probable, in fact, that if the United States did not take the islands, Spain would sell her vanishing equity in the property to some other power which possessed the equipment necessary to conquer the Philippines. To many this eventuality did not seem objectionable, as is indicated by the remark, already quoted, of an American official to certain Germans: "We don't want the Philippines; why don't you take them?" That this attitude was foolishly Quixotic is obvious, but more effective in the molding of public opinion was the feeling that it was cowardly.

In such a changing condition of public sentiment, McKinley was a better index of what the majority wanted than a referendum could have been. In August he stated: "I do not want any ambiguity to be allowed to remain on this point. The negotiators of both countries are the ones who shall resolve upon the permanent advantages which we shall ask in the archipelago, and decide upon the intervention, disposition, and government of the Philippines." His instructions to the commissioners actually went farther:

Avowing unreservedly the purpose which has animated all our effort, and still solicitous to adhere to it, we cannot be unmindful that, without any desire or design on our part, the war has brought us new duties and responsibilities which we must meet and discharge as becomes a great nation on whose growth and career from the beginning the Ruler of Nations has plainly written the high command and pledge of civilization.

Incidental to our tenure in the Philippines is the commercial opportunity to which American statesmanship cannot be indifferent. . . . Asking only the open door for ourselves, we are ready to accord the open door to others.

In view of what has been stated, the United States cannot accept less than the cession in full rights and sovereignty of the island of Luzon.

The American commissioners were divided. Day favored the limited terms of the instructions; Davis, Frye, and Reid wished the whole group of the Philippines; Gray emphatically protested against taking any part of the islands. On the 26th of October, Hay telegraphed that the President had decided that "the cession must be of the whole Archipelago or none." The Spanish commissioners objected strongly to this new development, and threatened to break off the negotiations which otherwise were practically concluded. This outcome would have put the United States in the unfortunate position of continuing a war which it had begun in the interests of Cuba for the quite different purpose of securing possession of the Philippines. The Spanish were probably not without hopes that under these changed conditions they might be able to bring to their active assistance that latent sympathy for them which existed so strongly in Europe. Nor was the basis of the claim of the United States entirely clear. On the 3d of November the American commissioners cabled to the President that they were convinced that the occupation of Manila did not constitute a conquest of the islands as a whole.

By this time, however, the President had decided that the United States must have the islands. On the 13th of November, Hay telegraphed that the United States was entitled to an indemnity for the cost of the war. This argument was not put forward because the United States wished indemnity but to give a technical basis for the American claim to the Philippines. In the same cablegram, Hay instructed the commissioners to offer Spain ten or twenty millions for all the islands. Upon this financial basis the treaty was finally concluded; it was signed on December 10, 1898; and ratifications were exchanged on April 11, 1899.

The terms of the treaty provided, first, for the relinquishment of sovereignty over Cuba by Spain. The island was to be occupied by the United States, in whose hands its subsequent disposition was left. All other Spanish islands in the West Indies, together with Guam in the Ladrones, were ceded to the United States. The whole archipelago of the Philippines, with water boundaries carefully but not quite accurately drawn, was ceded to the United States, which by the same article agreed to pay Spain $20,000,000. All claims for indemnity or damages between the two nations, or either nation and the citizens of the other, were mutually relinquished, the United States assuming the adjudication and settlement of all claims of her own citizens against Spain.

This treaty, even more than the act of war, marked a turning point in the relation of the United States to the outside world. So violent was the opposition of those who disapproved, and so great the reluctance of even the majority of those who approved, to acknowledge that the United States had emerged from the isolated path which it had been treading since 1823, that every effort was made to minimize the significance of the beginning of a new era in American history. It was argued by those delving into the past that the Philippines actually belonged to the Western Hemisphere because the famous demarcation line drawn by Pope Alexander VI, in 1493, ran to the west of them; it was, indeed, partly in consequence of that line that Spain had possessed the islands. Before Spain lost Mexico her Philippine trade had actually passed across the Pacific, through the Mexican port of Acapulco, and across the Atlantic. Yet these interesting historical facts were scarcely related in the mind of the public to the more immediate and tangible fact that the annexation of the Philippines gave the United States a far-flung territory situated just where all the powerful nations of the world were then centering their interest.

In opposition to those who disapproved of this extension of territory, it was argued more cogently that, in spite of the prevailing belief of the thirty preceding years, the United States had always been an expanding power, stretching its authority over new areas with a persistency and rapidity hardly equaled by any other nation, and that this latest step was but a new stride in the natural expansion of the United States. But here again the similarity between the former and the most recent steps was more apparent than real. Louisiana, Florida,

Texas, California, and Oregon, had all been parts of an obvious geographical whole. Alaska, indeed, was detached, but its acquisition had been partly accidental, and it was at least a part of the American continent and would, in the opinion of many, eventually become contiguous by the probable annexation of Canada. Moreover, none of the areas so far occupied by the United States had been really populated. It had been a logical expectation that American people would soon overflow these acquired lands and assimilate the inhabitants. In the case of the Philippines, on the other hand, it was fully recognized that Americans could at most be only a small governing class, and that even Porto Rico, accessible as it was, would prove too thickly settled to give hopes of Americanization.

The terms of the treaty with Spain, indeed, recognized these differences. In all previous instances, except Alaska, the added territory had been incorporated into the body of the United States with the expectation, now realized except in Hawaii, of reaching the position of self-governing and participating States of the Union. Even in the case of Alaska it had been provided that all inhabitants remaining in residence, except uncivilized Indians, should become citizens of the United

States. In the case of these new annexations resulting from the war with Spain, provision was made only for the religious freedom of the inhabitants. "The civil rights and political status of the native inhabitants of the territories hereby ceded to the United States shall be determined by the Congress." There could therefore be no doubt that for the first time the United States had acquired colonies and that the question whether they should develop into integral parts of the country or into dependencies of an imperialistic republic was left to the future to decide.

It was but natural that such striking events and important decisions should loom large as factors in the following presidential campaign. The Republicans endorsed the Administration, emphatically stated that the independence and self-government of Cuba must be secured, and, with reference to the other islands, declared that "the largest measure of self-government consistent with their welfare and our duties shall be secured to them by law." The Democrats asserted that "no nation can long endure half republic and half empire," and favored "an immediate declaration of the Nation's purpose to give the Filipinos, first, a stable form of government; second, independence; and third, protection from outside interference such as has been given for nearly a century to the republics of Central and South America." The Democrats were at a disadvantage owing to the fact that, since so much had been irrevocably accomplished, they could not raise the whole issue of colonial expansion but only advocate a different policy for the handling of what seemed to most people to be details. The distrust which their financial program of 1896 had excited, moreover, still hung over them and repelled many voters who might have supported them on questions of foreign and colonial policies. Nevertheless the reëlection of President McKinley by a greatly increased majority must be taken as indicating that the American people generally approved of his policies and accepted the momentous changes which had been brought about by the successful conclusion of the war with Spain.

# CHAPTER XIII

### A PEACE WHICH MEANT WAR

In a large way, ever since the Spanish War, the United States has been adjusting its policy to the world conditions of which that struggle first made the people aware. The period between 1898 and 1917 will doubtless be regarded by the historian a hundred years from now as a time of transition similar to that between 1815 and 1829. In that earlier period John Marshall and John Quincy Adams did much by their wisdom and judgment to preserve what was of value in the old régime for use in the new. In the later period John Hay performed, though far less completely, a somewhat similar function.

John Hay had an acquaintance with the best traditions of American statesmanship which falls to the lot of few men. He was private secretary to Lincoln during the Civil War, he had as his most intimate friend in later life Henry Adams, the historian, who lived immersed in the memories and traditions of a family which has taken a distinguished part in the Government of the United States from its beginning.   Possessed of an ample fortune, Hay had lived much abroad and in the society of the men who governed Europe.   He was experienced in newspaper work and in diplomacy, and he came to be Secretary of State fresh from a residence in England where as Ambassador he had enjoyed wide popularity.   With a lively wit and an engaging charm of manner, he combined a knowledge of international law and of history which few of our Secretaries have possessed.   Moreover he knew men and how to handle them.   Until the death of McKinley in 1901 he was left almost free in the administration of his office.   He once said that the President spoke to him of his office scarcely once a month.   In the years from 1901 to 1905 he worked under very different conditions, for President Roosevelt discussed affairs of state with him daily and took some matters entirely into his own hands.

Hay found somewhat better instruments to work with than most Americans were inclined to believe probable.   It is true that the American diplomatic service abroad has not always reflected credit upon the country.   It has contained extremely able and distinguished men but also many who have been stupid, ignorant, and ill-mannered. The State Department in Washington, however, has almost escaped the vicissitudes of politics and has been graced by the long and disinterested service of competent officials. From 1897 to 1913, moreover, the service abroad was built up on the basis of continuity and promotion.

One sign of a new epoch was the changed attitude of the American public toward annexation. While the war was in progress the United States yielded to the desires of Hawaii, and annexed the islands as a part of the United States, with the hope of their eventual statehood. In 1899 the United States consented to change the cumbrous and unsuccessful arrangement by which, in partnership with Great Britain and Germany, it had supervised the native government of Samoa. No longer unwilling to acquire distant territories, the United States took in full possession the island of Tutuila, with its harbor of Pago-Pago, and consented to Germany's taking the remainder of the islands, while Great Britain received compensation elsewhere. In 1900 the Government paid over to Spain $100,000 for Sibutú and Cagayan Sulú, two islands really belonging to the Philippines but overlooked in the treaty. Proud of the navy and with a new recognition of its necessities, the United States sought naval stations in those areas where the fleet might have to operate. In the Pacific the Government obtained Midway and Wake islands in 1900. In the West Indies, the harbor of Guantánamo was secured from Cuba, and in 1903 a treaty was made with Denmark for the purchase of her islands — which, however, finally became American possessions only in 1917.

By her policy toward Cuba, the United States gave the world a striking example of observing the plighted word even when contrary to the national interest. For a century the United States had expected to acquire the "Pearl of the Antilles." Spain in the treaty of peace refused to recognize the Cuban Government and relinquished the island into the hands of the United States. The withdrawal of the Spanish troops left the Cuban Government utterly unable to govern, and the United States was forced to occupy the island. Nevertheless the Government had begun the war with a recognition of Cuban independence and to that declaration it adhered. The country gave the best of its talent to make the islands self-governing as quickly as possible. Harvard University invited

Cuban teachers to be its guests at a summer session. American medical men labored with a martyr's devotion to stamp out disease. General Wood, as military governor, established order and justice and presided over the evolution of a convention assembled to draft a constitution for the people of Cuba and to determine the relations of the United States and Cuba. These relations, indeed, were already under consideration at Washington and were subsequently embodied in the Platt Amendment.[1] This measure directed the President to leave the control of Cuba to the people of the island as soon as they should agree to its terms. It also required that the Government of Cuba should never allow a foreign power to impair its independence; that it would contract no debt for which it could not provide a sinking fund from the ordinary revenue; that it would grant to the United States "lands necessary for coaling or naval stations"; that it would provide for the sanitation of its cities; and that the United States should have the right to intervene, "for the preservation of Cuban independence, the maintenance of a government adequate for the protection of life, property, and individual liberty, and for discharging" certain

[1] An amendment to the Army Appropriation Bill of March 2, 1901.

obligations with respect to Spanish subjects which the United States had assumed in the treaty signed at Paris. After some hesitation the convention added these provisions to the new constitution of Cuba. On May 20, 1902, the American troops withdrew, leaving Cuba in better condition than she had ever been before. Subsequently the United States was forced to intervene to preserve order, but, though the temptation was strong to remain, the American troops again withdrew after they had done their constructive work. The voluntary entrance of Cuba into the Great War in coöperation with the United States was a tribute to the generosity and honesty of the American people.

Porto Rico presented a problem different from that which the United States had to solve in Cuba. There existed no native organization which could supply even the basis for the formation of a government. The people seemed, indeed, to have no desire for independence, and public sentiment in the United States generally favored the permanent possession of the island. After a period of rule entirely at the discretion of the President, Congress established in 1900 a form of government based on that of the American territories. Porto Rico remained, however, unincorporated into the Union, and it was long doubtful whether it would remain a dependency or would ultimately attain statehood. In 1917, however, the degree of self-government was increased, and the inhabitants were made American citizens. It now seems probable that the island will ultimately become a State of the Union.

Meanwhile on the other side of the world the United States had a more unpleasant task. The revolted Filipinos, unlike the Cubans, had not declared themselves for independence but for redress of grievances. The United States had assisted Aguinaldo, at the moment in exile, to return to the islands after the Battle of Manila Bay but had not officially recognized him as having authority. When he saw Spanish power disappearing under American blows, he declared himself in favor of the abolition of all foreign rule. This declaration, of course, in no way bound the United States, to whom the treaty with Spain, the only recognized sovereign, ceded the island absolutely. There was no flaw in the title of the United States, and there were no obligations, save those of humanity, to bind the Americans in their treatment of the natives. Nevertheless, the great majority of Americans would doubtless have gladly favored a policy similar to that pursued in the case of Cuba, had it seemed in any way practicable. Unfortunately, however, the Filipinos did not constitute a nation but only a congeries of peoples and tribes of differing race and origin, whom nearly four centuries of Spanish rule had not been able to make live at peace with one another. Some were Christians, some Mohammedans, some heathen savages; some wore European clothes, some none at all. The particular tribe which formed the chief support of Aguinaldo, the Tagalogs, comprised less than one half of the population of the island of Luzon. The United States had taken the islands largely because it did not see any one else to whom it could properly shift the burden. The shoulders of the Tagalogs did not seem broad enough for the responsibility.

The United States prepared, therefore, to carry on the task which it had assumed, while Aguinaldo, with his army circling Manila, prepared to dispute its title. On February 4, 1899, actual hostilities broke out. By this time Aguinaldo had a capital at Malolos, thirty miles north of Manila, a government, thirty or forty thousand troops, and an influence which he was extending throughout the islands by means of secret organizations and superstitious appeals. This seemed a puny strength to put forth against the United States but various circumstances combined to make the contest less unequal than it seemed, and the outcome was probably more in doubt than that in the war with Spain.

The United States had at the moment but fourteen thousand men in the islands, under the command of General Otis. Some of these were volunteers who had been organized to fight Spain and who could not be held after the ratification of peace. Congress had, indeed, provided for an increase in the regular army, but not sufficient to provide the "40,000 effectives for the field," whom Otis had requested in August, 1899. There were, of course, plenty of men available in America for service in the Philippines, and finally twelve regiments of volunteers were raised, two of which were composed of negroes. Aguinaldo's strength lay in the configuration of the country, in its climate, which for four centuries had prevented a complete conquest by the Spaniards, and in the uncertainty which he knew existed as to how far the American people would support a war waged apparently for conquest, against the wishes of the Filipinos. On the other hand, the chief advantages of the American forces lay in Aguinaldo's lack of arms and in the power of the American

Navy, which confined the fighting for the most part to Luzon.

In March, General MacArthur began to move to the north, and on the last day of that month he entered Malolos. On the 23d of April he pushed farther northward toward Calumpit, where the Filipino generalissimo, Luna, had prepared a position which he declared to be impregnable. This brief campaign added a new favorite to the American roll of honor, for it was here that Colonel Funston, at the head of his gallant Kansans, crossed the rivers Bag-bag and Rio Grande, under circumstances that gave the individual American soldier a prestige in the eyes of the Filipinos and a reputation which often ran far ahead of the army.

General Luna had torn up the ties and rails of the steel railroad bridge over the Bag-bag, and had let down the span next the far bank. Thus cut off from attack by a deep river two hundred feet wide, the Filipino commander had entrenched his forces on the farther side. Shielded by fields of young corn and bamboo thickets, the Americans approached the bank of the river. A naval gun on an armored train bombarded the Filipinos but could not silence their trenches. It was therefore necessary to cross on the bridge, and under fire. General Wheaton ordered Colonel Funston to seize the bridge. With about ten men Funston rushed the nearer end which stood in the open. Working themselves along the girders, the men finally reached the broken span. Beyond that, swimming was the only method of reaching the goal. Leaving their guns behind them, Colonel Funston and three others swung themselves off the bridge and into the stream. Quite unarmed, the four landed and rushed the nearest trenches. Fortunately these had been abandoned under American fire, and rifles and cartridges had been left behind. Thus this aquatic charge by unarmed men secured the bridge and enabled the American troops to cross.

Not far beyond was the Rio Grande, four hundred feet broad and crossed by another railroad bridge that must be taken. Here again the task was entrusted to Colonel Funston and the Twentieth Kansas. This time they found an old raft. Two privates stripped and swam across with a rope. Landing unarmed on the enemy's side of the river, they fastened their rope to a part of the very trench works of the Filipinos. With this connection established, Colonel Funston improvised a ferry and was soon on the enemy's side with supports. A stiff, unequal fight remained, as the ferry carried but six men on each trip. The bank was soon won, however, and the safe crossing of the army was assured. Such acts gave the natives a respect for Americans as fighting men, which caused it to be more and more difficult for the Filipino commanders to bring their forces to battle in the open.

General Lawton in the meantime was conducting a brilliant movement to the eastward. After breaking the enemy forces, he returned to Manila and then marched southward into the Tagalog country, where on the 13th of June, at Zapoti Bridge, he won the most stoutly contested battle of the insurrection. The successful conclusion of these operations brought the most civilized part of the island under American control.

The fighting now became scattered and assumed gradually a guerrilla character. The abler commanders of the American forces found their way to the top, and the troops, with their natural adaptability, constantly devised new methods of meeting new situations. A war of strangely combined mountain and sea fighting, involving cavalry and infantry and artillery, spread over the islands in widening circles and met with lessening resistance. An indication of the new character of the war was given by the change of the military organization, in April, 1900, from one of divisions and brigades, to a geographical basis. Each commander was now given charge of a certain area and used his men to reduce this district to order.

The insurgents fought in small groups and generally under local chieftains. Their advantage lay in their thorough knowledge of the country and in the sympathy of a part of the population and the fear of another part, for outlaws living in concealment and moving in the dark can often inspire a terror which regular troops under discipline fail to engender. The Americans could not trust the natives, as it was impossible to tell the truthful from the treacherous. Nevertheless it was a kind of fighting which gave unusual scope for that American individualism, so strongly represented in the army, to which the romance of precisely this sort of thing had drawn just the class of men best fitted for the work. Scouting, counter scouting, surprise attacks, and ambuscades formed the daily news transmitted from the front — affairs not of regiments and companies but of squads and individuals. When face to face, however, the Filipinos seldom stood their ground, and the American ingenuity and eager willingness to attempt any new thing gradually got the better of the local

knowledge and unscrupulousness as to the laws of
war which had at first given the natives an advantage. Funston, now Brigadier General, and his
"suicide squad" continued to play an active
part, but a similar spirit of daring and ingenuity
pervaded the whole army.

Broken as were the Filipino field forces and
widening as was the area of peace, the result of
the island campaign was still uncertain. It rested
upon two unknown quantities. The first was the
nature of the Filipinos. Would they remain ir-
reconcilable, ever ready to take advantage of a moment of weakness? If such were to be the case,
we could look for no real conquest, but only a forcible occupation, which the people of the United
States would never consent to maintain. The
second unknown quantity was the American people
themselves. Would they sustain the occupation
sufficiently long to give a reasonable test of the
possibilities of success?

Two events brought these uncertainties to an
end. In the first place, William Jennings Bryan
was defeated for the presidency in November, 1900,
and President McKinley was given four more years
in which to complete the experiment. In the second
place, on March 23, 1901, Aguinaldo, who had been

long in concealment, was captured. Though there had long been no possibility of really commanding the insurgent forces as a whole, Aguinaldo had remained the center of revolt and occasionally showed his hand, as in the attempt to negotiate a peace on the basis of independence. In February an intercepted letter had given a clue to his hiding place. Funston, in spite of his new rank, determined personally to undertake the capture. The signature of Lacuna, one of the insurgent leaders, was forged and letters were sent to Aguinaldo informing him of the capture of five Americans, who were being sent to headquarters. Among the five was Funston himself. The "insurgent" guard, clad in captured uniforms, consisted for the most part of Macabebes, hereditary enemies of the Tagalogs — for the Americans had now learned the Roman trick of using one people against another. The ruse succeeded perfectly. The guard and its supposed prisoners were joyfully received by Aguinaldo, but the tables were quickly turned and Aguinaldo's capture was promptly effected.

On the 19th of April, Aguinaldo wrote: "After mature deliberation, I resolutely proclaim to the world that I cannot refuse to heed the voice of a people longing for peace, nor the lamentations of thousands of families yearning to see their dear ones enjoying the liberty and promised generosity of the great American nation. By acknowledging and accepting the sovereignty of the United States throughout the Philippine Archipelago, as I now do, and without any reservation whatsoever, I believe that I am serving thee, my beloved country."

On the 19th of May, General Wheaton, Chief of Staff in the Philippines, sent the following dispatch to Washington: "Lacuna having surrendered with all his officers and men today, I report that all insurrectionary leaders in this department have been captured or have surrendered. This is the termination of the state of war in this department so far as armed resistance to the authority of the United States is concerned."

There was subsequent fighting with other tribes and in other islands, particularly with the Moros of the Sulu group, but by the time Aguinaldo had accepted American rule, the uncertainty of the American people had been resolved, and the execution of the treaty with Spain had been actually accomplished. As seventy thousand troops were no longer needed in the islands, the volunteers and many of the regulars were sent home, and there began an era of peace such as the Philippines had never before known.

During the suppression of the insurrection the American Army had resorted to severe measures, though they by no means went to the extremes that were reported in the press. It was realized, however, that the establishment of a permanent peace must rest upon an appeal to the good will and self-interest of the natives. The treatment of the conquered territories, therefore, was a matter of the highest concern not only with reference to the public opinion at home but to the lasting success of the military operations which had just been concluded.

There was as yet no law in the United States relating to the government of dependencies. The entire control of the islands therefore rested, in the first instance, with the President and was vested by him, subject to instructions, in the Military Governor. The army fortunately reflected fully the democratic tendencies of the United States as a whole. In June, 1899, General Lawton encouraged and assisted the natives in setting up in their villages governing bodies of their own selection. In August, he issued a general order, based upon a law of the islands, providing for a general system of

local government into which there was introduced
for the first time the element of really popular elec-
tion. In 1900, a new code of criminal procedure,
largely the work of Enoch Herbert Crowder, at
that time Military Secretary, was promulgated,
which surrounded the accused with practically all
the safeguards to which the Anglo-Saxon is accustomed except jury trial, for which the people
were unprepared.

To advise with regard to a permanent system of
government for the Philippines President McKinley appointed in January, 1899, a commission con-
sisting of Jacob G. Schurman, President of Cornell
University, Dean C. Worcester, who had long been
engaged in scientific research in the Philippines,
Colonel Charles Denby, for many years previously
minister to China, Admiral Dewey, and General
E. S. Otis. Largely upon their recommendation,
the President appointed a second commission,
headed by Judge William Howard Taft to carry on
the work of organizing civil government which had
already begun under military direction and gradually to take over the legislative power. The Military Governor was to continue to exercise executive power. In 1901, Congress at length took action,
vesting all military, civil, and judicial powers in

such persons as the President might appoint to govern the islands. McKinley immediately appointed Judge Taft to the new governorship thus authorized. In 1901 in the "Insular Cases" the Supreme Court also gave its sanction to what had been done. In legislation for the territories, it held that Congress was not bound by all the restrictions of the Constitution, as, for instance, that requiring jury trial; that Porto Rico and the Philippines were neither foreign countries nor completely parts of the United States, though Congress was at liberty to incorporate them into the Union.

There was, however, no disposition to incorporate the Philippines into the United States, but there has always been a widespread sentiment that the islands should ultimately be given their independence, and this sentiment has largely governed the American attitude toward them. A native Legislature was established in 1907 under Governor Taft,[1] and under the Wilson Administration the process toward independence has been accelerated, and

[1] By the Act of July 1, 1902, the Legislature was to consist of two houses, the Commission acting as an upper house and an elective assembly constituting a lower house. The Legislature at its first session was to elect two delegates who were to sit, without the right to vote, in the House of Representatives at Washington. An Act of August 29, 1916, substituted an elective Senate for the Philippine Commission as the upper house of the Legislature.

dates begin to be considered. The process of preparation for independence has been threefold: the development of the physical well-being of the islands, the education of the islanders, and the gradual introduction of the latter into responsible positions of government. With little of the encouragement which might have come from appreciative interest at home, thousands of Americans have now labored in the Philippines for almost twenty years, but with little disposition to settle there permanently. Their efforts to develop the Filipinos have achieved remarkable success. It has of late been found possible to turn over such a large proportion of the governmental work to the natives that the number of Americans in the islands is steadily diminishing. The outbreak of the war with Germany found the natives loyal to American interests and even saw a son of Aguinaldo taking service under the Stars and Stripes. Such a tribute, like the services of Generals Smuts and Botha to Great Britain, compensates for the friction and noise with which democracy works and is the kind of triumph which carries reassurance of its ultimate efficiency and justice.

# CHAPTER XIV

## THE OPEN DOOR

THE United States arrived in the Orient at a moment of high excitement. Russia was consolidating the advance of two centuries by the building of the trans-Siberian railroad, and was looking eagerly for a port in the sun, to supplement winter-bound Vladivostok. Great Britain still regarded Russia as the great enemy and, pursuing her policy of placing buffer states between her territories and her enemies, was keenly interested in preventing any encroachment southward which might bring the Russian bear nearer India. France, Russia's ally, possessed Indo-China, which was growing at the expense of Siam and which might grow northwards into China. Germany saw in eastern Asia the richest prize remaining in the world not yet possessed by her rivals, and it was for this that she was seeking power in the Pacific. Having missed the Philippines, she quickly secured Samoa and purchased from Spain the Caroline Islands, east of the Philippines, and all that the United States had not taken of Spain's empire in the Pacific.

These latent rivalries had been brought into the open by the Chino-Japanese War of 1894–1895, which showed the powerlessness of China. The western world was, indeed, divided in opinion as to whether this colossus of the East was essentially rotten, old, decrepit, and ready to disintegrate, or was merely weak because of arrested development, which education and training could correct. At any rate, China was regarded as sick and therefore became for the moment even more interesting than Turkey, the traditional sick man of Europe. If China were to die, her estate would be divided. If he were really to revitalize her vast bulk by adapting her millions to modern ways, she had but to stretch herself and the toilfully acquired Asiatic possessions of the European powers would shiver to pieces; and if she awoke angry, Europe herself might well tremble. The really wise saw that the important thing was to determine the kind of education which China should receive, and in solving this problem the palm of wisdom must be given to the missionaries who represented the great Christian societies of Europe and America. To small-minded statesmen it seemed that the situation called for conquest. No nation was willing to be late at the division, if division it was to be; while if China was to awake, the European powers felt that she should awake shackled. By no one was this latter view so clearly held as by the Kaiser. With his accustomed versatility, he designed a cartoon showing the European powers, armed and with Germania in the forefront, confronting the yellow peril. On sending his troops to China in 1900, he told them to imitate the methods of the Huns, in order to strike lasting terror to the heart of the yellow race. By such means he sought to direct attention to the menace of the Barbarian when he was himself first stating that doctrine of Teutonic frightfulness which has proved, in our day at least, to be the real world peril.

It was Japan who had exposed the weakness of the giant, but her victory had been so easy that her own strength was as yet untested. Japan had come of age in 1894 when, following the example of Great Britain, the various powers had released her from the obligation of exterritoriality imposed upon her by treaties when their subjects were unwilling to trust themselves to her courts. It was still uncertain, however, whether the assumption

European methods by Japan was real, and her position as a great power was not yet established. In the very moment of her triumph over China she was forced to submit to the humiliation of having the terms of peace supervised by a concert of powers and of having many of the spoils of her victory torn from her.

The chief fruits that remained to Japan from her brilliant military victory were Formosa and the recognition of the separation of Korea from China. These acquisitions gave her an opportunity to show her capacity for real expansion, but whether she would be able to hold her prize was yet to be proven. The European states, however, claimed that by the Japanese victories the balance of power in the Orient had been upset and that it must be adjusted. The obvious method was for each power to demand something for itself. In 1898 Germany secured a lease of Kiao-chau Bay across the Yellow Sea from Korea, which she at once fortified and where she proceeded to develop a port with the hope of commanding the trade of all that part of China. Russia in the same way secured, somewhat farther to the north, Port Arthur and Talien-wan, and proceeded to build Dalny as the commercial outlet of her growing railroad. Great

Britain immediately occupied Wei-hai-wei, which
was midway between the German and Russian bases
and commanded from the south the entrance to
Pekin, and also, much farther to the south, Mirs
Bay, which gave security to her commercial center
at Hong-kong. France took Kwang-chau, still farther to the south, and Italy received Sanmen, somewhat to the south of the Yangtsze-kiang. From
these ports each power hoped to extend a sphere o
influence. It was axiomatic that such a sphere
would be most rapidly developed and most solidly
held if special tariff regulations were devised to
throw the trade into the hands of the merchant
of the nation holding the port. The next step
therefore, in establishing the solidity of an Asiatic base, would be the formulation of specia
tariffs. The result would be the practical division
of China into districts having different and opposed
commercial interests.

The United States did not arrive in this energeti
company as an entire stranger. With both Chin
and Japan her relations had long been intimate and
friendly. American merchants had traded ginseng
and furs for China silks and teas ever since th
United States had been a nation. In 1786 the
Government had appointed a commercial agent a

Canton and in 1844 had made one of the first commercial treaties with China. In 1854 the United States had been the point of the foreign wedge that opened Japan to western civilization and inaugurated that amazing period of national reorganization and assimilation which has given the Japanese Empire her place in the world today. American missionaries had labored long and disinterestedly for the moral regeneration of both China and Japan with results which are now universally recognized as beneficial, though in 1900 there was still among the Chinese much of that friction which is the inevitable reaction from an attempt to change the fundamentals of an ancient faith and long-standing habits. American merchants, it is true, had been of all classes, but at any rate there had always been a sufficient leaven of those of the highest type to insure a reasonable reputation.

The conduct of the American Government in the Far East had been most honorable and friendly. The treaty with Japan in 1858 contained the clause: "The President of the United States, at the request of the Japanese Government, will act as a friendly mediator in such matters of difference as may arise between the Government of Japan and any European power." Under Seward the United States

did, indeed, work in concert with European power
to force the opening of the Shimonoseki Straits in
1864, and a revision of the tariff in 1866. Sub
sequently, however, the United States coöperate
with Japan in her effort to free herself from certain
disadvantageous features of early treaties. In 188
the United States returned the indemnity receive
at the time of the Shimonoseki affair — an exampl
of international equity almost unique at the tim
but subsequently paralleled in American relation
with China. The one serious difficulty existing i
the relationships of the United States with bot
China and Japan resulted from an unwillingness t
receive their natives as immigrants when people o
nearly every other country were admitted. Th
American attitude had already been expressed i
the Chinese Exclusion Act. As yet the chief diff
culty was with that nation, but it was inevitable tha
such distinctions would prove particularly gallin
to the rising spirit of the Japanese.

John Hay was keenly aware of the possibi
ties involved in these Far Eastern events. Of pr
found moment under any circumstances, they we
doubly so now that the United States was terr
torially involved. To take a slice of this Easter
area was a course quite open to the United Stat

and one which some of the powers at least would
have welcomed.  Hay, however, wrote to Paul
Dana on March 16, 1899, as follows: "We are, of
course, opposed to the dismemberment of that empire [China], and we do not think that the public
opinion of the United States would justify this
Government in taking part in the great game of
spoliation now going on."   He felt also that the
United States should not tie its hands by "formal
alliances with other Powers interested," nor was
he prepared "to assure China that we would join
her in repelling that demand by armed force."

It remained, then, for the Secretary of State to
find a lever for peaceful interference on the part of
his country and a plan for future operations.   The
first he found in the commercial interest of the
United States.   Since the Government refrained
from pressing for special favors in any single part
of the Chinese Empire, it could demand that American interests be not infringed anywhere.   The
Secretary of State realized that in a democracy
statesmen cannot overlook the necessity of con-
densing their policies into popular catchwords or
slogans.   Today such phrases represent in large
measure the power referred to in the old saying:
"Let me make the songs of a nation, and I care not

who makes its laws." The single phrase, "scrap
of paper," probably cost Germany more than any
one of her atrocious deeds in the Great War. Hay's
policy with regard to China had the advantage of
two such phrases. The "golden rule," however
proved less lasting than the "open door," which
was coined apparently in the instructions to the
Paris Peace Commission. This phrase expressed
just what the United States meant. The precise
plan of the American Government was outlined
and its execution undertaken in a circular note of
September 6, 1899, which the Secretary of State addressed to London, Berlin, and St. Petersburg. In
this he asked the powers to agree to respect all
existing open ports and established interests within their respective spheres, to enforce the Chinese
tariff and no other, and to refrain from all discrimination in port and railroad charges. To make
such a proposal to the European powers required
courage. In its essential elements the situation in
the Far East was not unlike the internal economic
condition prevailing at the same time in the
United States. In this country great transportation monopolies had been built up, having an enormous capitalization, and many of them were dependent for their profits on the advantage of price

fixing that monopoly may be expected to bring. Then state and nation stepped in and asserted their right to fix prices in the interest of the consumer. The consequent political struggles illustrate the difficulties besetting the Secretary of State in his somewhat similar attempt to take the chief fruits from the powers which had just acquired Chinese territory — an undertaking in which he had none of the support of legal powers effective in the United States.

That Hay so promptly succeeded in putting at least a toe in the door which he wished to open was due to a number of circumstances. Great Britain, devoted to the principle of free trade, heartily approved of his proposal and at once accepted its terms. The other powers expressed their sympathy with the ideas of the note, but, in the case of Russia at least, without the faintest intention of paying any heed to it. Hay promptly notified each power of the others' approval and stated that, with this unanimous consent, he would regard its acceptance of the proposals as "final and definitive."

The force which Hay had used was the moral influence of world opinion. None of the powers dared, with its hands fresh filled with Chinese plunder, openly to assert that it had taken the spoils for selfish reasons alone — at least, after another power had denied such purpose. Hay saw and capitalized the force of conventional morality which, however superficial in many cases, had influenced the European powers, particularly since the time of the Holy Alliance. Accustomed to clothe their actions in the garb of humanitarianism, they were not, when caught thus red-handed, prepared to be a mark of scorn for the rest of the world. The cult of unabashed might was still a closet philosophy which even Germany, its chief devotee, was not yet ready to avow to the world. Of course Hay knew that the battle was not won, for the bandits still held the booty. He was too wise to attempt to wrench it from them, for that indeed would have meant battle for which the United States was not prepared in military strength or popular intention. He had merely pledged these countries to use their acquisitions for the general good. Though the promises meant little in themselves, to have exacted them was an initial step toward victory.

In the meantime the penetration of foreign influences into China was producing a reaction. A wave of protest against the "foreign devils" swept through the population and acquired intensity

**from** the acts of fanatic religious leaders. That strange character, the Dowager Empress, yielded to the "Boxers," who obtained possession of Pekin, cut off the foreigners from the outside world, and besieged them in the legations. That some such movement was inevitable must have been apparent to many European statesmen, and that it would give them occasion, by interference and punishment, to solidify their "spheres of influence" must have occurred to them. The "open door" was in as immediate peril as were the diplomats in Pekin.

Secretary Hay did not, however, yield to these altered circumstances. Instead, he built upon the leadership which he had assumed. He promptly accepted the international responsibility which the emergency called for. The United States at once agreed to take its share, in coöperation with the Great Powers, in whatever measures should be judged necessary. The first obvious measure was to relieve the foreign ministers who were besieged in Pekin. American assistance was active and immediate. By the efforts of the American Government, communication with the legations was opened; the American naval forces were soon at Tientsin, the port of Pekin; and five or six thousand troops were hastily sent from the Philippines. The United

States therefore bore its full proportion of the task. The largest contingent of the land forces was, indeed, from Germany, and the command of the whole undertaking was by agreement given to the German commander, Graf von Waldersee. Owing, however, to his remoteness from the scene of action, he did not arrive until after Pekin had been reached and the relief of the legations, which was the first if not the main object of the expedition, had been accomplished. After this, the resistance of the Chinese greatly decreased and the country was practically at the mercy of the concert of powers.

By thus bearing its share in the responsibilities of the situation, the United States had won a vote in determining the result. Secretary Hay, however, had not waited for the military outcome, and he aimed not at a vote in the concert of powers but at its leadership. While the international expedition was gathering its forces, he announced in a circular note that "the policy of the Government of the United States is to seek a solution which may bring about permanent safety and peace to China, preserve Chinese territorial and administrative entity, protect all rights guaranteed to friendly powers by treaty and international law, and safeguard for the world the principle of equal and impartial trade with all parts of the Chinese Empire." To this position he requested the powers to assent.

Again Hay had hit upon a formula which no self-respecting power could deny. Receiving from practically all a statement of their purpose to preserve the "integrity" of China and the "Open Door" just when they were launching the greatest military movement ever undertaken in the Far East by the western world, he made it impossible to turn punishment into destruction and partition. The legations were saved and so was China. After complicated negotiations an agreement was reached which exacted heavy pecuniary penalties, and in the case of Germany, whose minister had been assassinated, a conspicuous and what was intended to be an enduring record of the crime and its punishment. China, however, remained a nation — with its door open.

Once more in 1904 the fate of China, and in fact that of the whole Far East, was thrown into the ring. Japan and Russia entered into a war which had practically no cause except the collision of their advancing interests in Chinese territory. Every land battle of the war, except those of the Saghalien campaign, was fought in China, Chinese ports were blockaded, Chinese waters were filled with

enemy mines and torpedoes, and the prize was
Chinese territory or territory recently taken from
her. To deny these facts was impossible; to admit them seemed to involve the disintegration of
the empire. Here again Secretary Hay, devising
a middle course, gained by his promptness of action the prestige of having been the first to speak.
On February 8, 1904, he asked Germany, Great
Britain, and France to join with the United States
in requesting Japan and Russia to recognize the
neutrality of China, and to localize hostilities within fixed limits. On January 10, 1905, remembering
how the victory of Japan in 1894 had brought com-
pensatory grants to all the powers, he sent out a
circular note expressing the hope on the part of the
American Government that the war would not
result in any "concession of Chinese territory to
neutral powers." Accustomed now to these invi-
tations which decency forbade them to refuse, all
the powers assented to this suggestion. The results of the war, therefore, were confined to Manchuria, and Japan promised that her occupation
of that province should be temporary and that commercial opportunity therein should be the same
for all. The culmination of American prestige
came with President Roosevelt's offer of the good

offices of the United States, on June 8, 1905. As a result, peace negotiations were concluded in the Treaty of Portsmouth (New Hampshire) in 1905. For this conspicuous service to the cause of peace President Roosevelt was awarded the Nobel prize.

Secretary Hay had therefore, in the seven years following the real arrival of the United States in the Far East, evolved a policy which was clear and definite, and one which appealed to the American people. While it constituted a variation from the precise methods laid down by President Monroe in 1823, in that it involved concerted and equal co-operation with the great powers of the world, Hay's policy rested upon the same fundamental bases: a belief in the fundamental right of nations to determine their own government, and the reduction to a minimum of intervention by foreign powers. To have refused to recognize intervention at all would have been, under the circumstances, to abandon China to her fate. In protecting its own right to trade with her, the United States protected the integrity of China. Hay had, moreover, so ably conducted the actual negotiations that the United States enjoyed for the moment the leadership in the concert of powers and exercised an authority more in accord with her potential than with her actual strength.

Secretary Hay's death in 1905 brought American leadership to an end, for, though his policies continued to be avowed by all concerned, their application was thereafter restricted. The integrity of Chinese territory was threatened, though not actually violated, by the action of Great Britain in Tibet and of Japan in Manchuria. Japan, recognized as a major power since her war with Russia, seemed in the opinion of many to leave but a crack of the door open in Manchuria, and her relationship with the United States grew difficult as she resented more and more certain discriminations against her citizens which she professed to find in the laws of some of the American States, particularly in those of California.

In 1908 Elihu Root, who succeeded Hay as Secretary of State, effected an understanding with Japan. Adopting a method which has become rather habitual in the relationship between the United States and Japan, Root and the Japanese ambassador exchanged notes. In these they both pointed out that their object was the peaceful development of their commerce in the Pacific; that "the policy of both governments, uninfluenced by any aggressive tendencies, is directed to the maintenance of the existing *status quo* in the region above mentioned, and to the defense of the principle of equal opportunity for commerce and industry in China"; that they both stood for the independence and integrity of China; and that, should any event threaten the stability of existing conditions, "it remained for the two governments to communicate with each other in order to arrive at an understanding as to what measures they may consider it useful to take."

The immigration problem between Japan and the United States was even more serious than that of the open door and the integrity of China. The teeming population of Japan was swarming beyond her island empire, and Korea and Manchuria did not seem to offer sufficient opportunity. The number of Japanese immigrants to this country, which before the Spanish War had never reached 2000 in any one year, now rose rapidly until in 1907 it reached 30,226. American sentiment, which had been favorable to Japan during her war with Russia, began to change. The public and particularly the laboring classes in the West, where most of the Japanese remained, objected to this increasing immigration, while a number of leaders of American opinion devoted themselves to converting the public to a belief that the military ambitions

of Japan included the Philippines and possibly
Hawaii, where the Japanese were a formidable element in the population.   As a consequence there
arose a strong demand that the principles of the
Chinese Exclusion Act be applied to the Japanese.
The situation was made more definite by the fact
that the board of education in San Francisco ruled
in 1906 that orientals should receive instruction in
special schools.  The Japanese promptly protested,
and their demand for their rights under the treaty
of 1894 was supported by the Tokio Government.
The international consequences of thus discriminat-
ing against the natives of so rising and self-confident
a country as Japan, and one conscious of its military
strength, were bound to be very different from the
difficulties encountered in the case of China.   The
United States confronted a serious situation, but fortunately did not confront it alone.   Australia and
British Columbia, similarly threatened by Japanese
immigration, were equally opposed to it.

Out of deference to Great Britain, with which she
had been allied since 1902, Japan consented that
her immigrants should not force their way into unwilling communities.   This position facilitated an
arrangement between the United States and Japan,
and an informal agreement was made in 1907.   The

schools of San Francisco were to be open to orien-
tal children not over sixteen years of age, while
Japan was to withhold passports from laborers who
planned to emigrate to the United States. This
plan has worked with reasonable success, but minor
issues have kept alive in both countries the bad
feeling on the subject. Certain States, particularly California, have passed laws, especially with
regard to the ownership and leasing of farm lands,
apparently intended to discriminate against Japanese who were already residents. These laws Japan
has held to be violations of her treaty provision for
consideration on the "most favored nation" basis,
and she has felt them to be opposed in spirit to the
"gentlemen's agreement" of 1907. The inability
of the Federal Government to control the policy
of individual States is not accepted by foreign
countries as releasing the United States from international obligations, so that, although friendly
agreements between the two countries were reached
on the major points, cause for popular irritation
still remained.

Philander C. Knox, who succeeded Root as
Secretary of State, devoted his attention rather to
the fostering of American interests in China than
to the development of the general policies of his

Department. While he refrained from asking for an American sphere of influence, he insisted that American capitalists obtain their fair share of the concessions for railroad building, mining, and other enterprises which the Chinese Government thought it necessary to give in order to secure capital for her schemes of modernization. As these concessions were supposed to carry political influence in the areas to which they applied, there was active rivalry for them, and Russia and Japan, which had no surplus capital, even borrowed in order to secure a share. This situation led to a tangled web of intrigue, perhaps inevitable but decidedly contrary to the usual American diplomatic habits; and at this game the United States did not prove particularly successful. In 1911 there broke out in China a republican revolution which was speedily successful. The new Government, as yet unrecognized, needed money, and the United States secured a share in a six-power syndicate which was organized to float a national loan. The conditions upon which this syndicate insisted, however, were as much political as they were pecuniary, and the new Government refused to accept them.

On the accession of President Wilson, the United States promptly led the way in recognizing the new republic in China. On March 18, 1913, the President announced: "The conditions of the loan seem to us to touch nearly the administrative independence of China itself; and this administration does not feel that it ought, even by implication, to be a party to those conditions." The former American policy of non-interference was therefore renewed, but it still remained uncertain whether the entrance of the United States into Far Eastern politics would do more than serve to delay the European dominance which seemed to be impending in 1898.

# CHAPTER XV

## THE PANAMA CANAL

WHILE American troops were threading the mountain passes and the morasses of the Philippines, scaling the walls of Pekin, and sunning themselves in the delectable pleasances of the Forbidden City, and while American Secretaries of State were penning dispatches which determined the fate of countries on the opposite side of the globe, the old diplomatic problems nearer home still persisted. The Spanish War, however, had so thoroughly changed the relationship of the United States to the rest of the world that the conditions under which even these old problems were to be adjusted or solved gave them entirely new aspects. The American people gradually but effectually began to take foreign affairs more seriously. As time went on, the Government made improvements in the consular and diplomatic services. Politicians found that their irresponsible threatenings of other countries had ceased to be politically profitable when public opinion realized what was at stake. Other countries, moreover, began to take the United States more seriously. The open hostility which they had shown on the first entrance of this nation into world politics changed, on second thought, to a desire on their part to placate and perhaps to win the support of this new and formidable power.

The attitude of Germany in particular was conspicuous. The Kaiser sent his brother, Prince Henry, to visit the United States. He presented the nation with a statue of Frederick the Great and Harvard with a Germanic museum; he ordered a Herreshoff yacht, and asked the President's daughter, Alice Roosevelt, to christen it; he established exchange professorships in the universities; and he began a campaign aimed apparently at securing for Germany the support of the entire American people, or, failing that, at organizing for German purposes the German-born element within the United States. France sought to revive the memory of her friendship for the United States during the Revolution by presenting the nation with a statue of Rochambeau, and she also established exchange professorships. In England, Cecil Rhodes, with his great dream of drawing together all portions of the British race, devoted his fortune to making Oxford the mold where all its leaders of thought and action should be shaped; and Joseph Chamberlain and other English leaders talked freely and enthusiastically of an alliance between Great Britain and the United States as the surest foundation for world peace.

It need not be supposed, however, that these international amenities meant that the United States was to be allowed to have its own way in the world. The friendliness of Great Britain was indeed sincere. Engaged between 1899 and 1902 in the Boer War, she appreciated ever more strongly the need for the friendship of the United States, and she looked with cordial approbation upon the development of Secretary Hay's policy in China. The British, however, like the Americans, are legalistically inclined, and disputes between the two nations are likely to be maintained to the limit of the law. The advantage of this legal mindedness is that there has always been a disposition in both peoples to submit to judicial award when ordinary negotiations have reached a deadlock. But the real affection for each other which underlay the eternal bickerings of the two nations had as yet not revealed itself to the

American consciousness. As most of the disputes of the United States had been with Great Britain, Americans were always on the alert to maintain all their claims and were suspicious of "British gold."

It was, therefore, in an atmosphere by no means conducive to yielding on the part of the United States, though it was one not antagonistic to good feeling, that the representatives of the two countries met. John Hay and Sir Julian Pauncefote, whose long quiet service in this country had made him the first popular British ambassador, now set about clearing up the problems confronting the two peoples. The first question which pressed for settlement was one of boundary. It had already taken ninety years to draw the line from the Atlantic to the Pacific, and now the purchase of Alaska by the United States had added new uncertainties to the international boundary. The claims of both nations were based on a treaty of 1825 between Great Britain and Russia. Like most attempts to define boundaries running through unexplored territories, the treaty terms admitted of two interpretations. The boundary line from Portland Channel to Mount St. Elias was stipulated to run everywhere a distance of ten marine leagues from the coast and to follow its sinuosities. This particular coast, however, is bitten into by long fiords stretching far into the country. Great Britain held that these were not part of the sea in the sense of the treaty and that the line should cut across them ten marine leagues from the outer coast line. On the other hand, the United States held that the line should be drawn ten marine leagues from the heads of these inlets. The discovery of gold on the Yukon in 1897 made this boundary question of practical moment. Action now became an immediate necessity. In 1899 the two countries agreed upon a *modus vivendi* and in 1903 arranged an arbitration. The arbitrating board consisted of three members from each of the two nations. The United States appointed Senator Henry Cabot Lodge, ex-Senator George Turner, and Elihu Root, then Secretary of War. Great Britain appointed two Canadians, Louis A. Jetté and A. B. Aylesworth, and Lord Alverstone, Chief Justice of England. Their decision was in accordance with the principle for which the United States had contended, though not following the actual line which it had sketched. It gave the Americans, however, full control of the coast and its harbors, and the settlement provided a mutually accepted boundary on every frontier.

With the discovery of gold in the far North

Alaska began a period of development which is rapidly making that territory an important economic factor in American life. Today the time when this vast northern coast was valuable only as the breeding ground for the fur seal seems long past. Nevertheless the fur seal continued to be sought, and for years the international difficulty of protecting the fisheries remained. Finally, in 1911, the United States entered into a joint agreement with Great Britain, Japan, and Russia, which is actually serving as a sort of international game law. The problems of Alaska that remain are therefore those of internal development.

Diplomacy, however, is not concerned solely with sensational episodes. American ministers and the State Department are engaged for the most part in the humdrum adjustment of minor differences which never find their way into the newspapers. Probably more such cases arise with Great Britain, in behalf of Canada, than with any other section of the globe. On the American continent rivers flow from one country into the other; railroads carry goods across the border and back again; citizens labor now in one country, now in the other; corporations do business in both. All these ties not only bind but chafe and give rise to constant negotiation. More and more

Great Britain has left the handling of such matters to the Canadian authorities, and, while there can be no interchange of ministers, there is an enormous transaction of business between Ottawa and Washington.

While there has of late years been little talk of annexation, there have been many in both countries who have desired to reduce the significance of the boundary to a minimum. This feeling led in 1911 to the formulation of a reciprocity agreement, which Canada, however, was unwilling to accept. Yet, if tariff restrictions were not removed, other international barriers were as far as possible done away with. In 1898 a commission was appointed to agree upon all points of difference. Working slowly but steadily, the commissioners settled one question after another, until practically all problems were put upon a permanent working basis. Perhaps the most interesting of the results of this activity was the appointment in 1908 of a permanent International Fisheries Commission, which still regulates that vexing question.

Another source of international complication arose out of the Atlantic fisheries off Newfoundland, which is not part of Canada. It is off these shores that the most important deep-sea fishing takes place. This fishery was one of the earliest American sources of wealth, and for nearly two centuries formed a sort of keystone of the whole commercial life of the United States. When in 1783 Great Britain recognized American independence, she recognized also that American fishermen had certain rights off these coasts. These rights, however, were not sufficient for the conduct of the fisheries, and so in addition certain "liberties" were granted, which allowed American fishers to land for the purpose of drying fish and of doing other things not generally permitted to foreigners. These concessions in fact amounted to a joint participation with the British. The rights were permanent, but the privileges were regarded as having lapsed after the War of 1812. In 1818 they were partially renewed, certain limited privileges being conceded. Ever since that date the problem of securing the additional privileges desired has been a subject for discussion between Great Britain and the United States. Between 1854 and 1866 the American Government secured them by reciprocity; between 1872 and 1884 it bought them; after 1888 it enjoyed them by a temporary *modus vivendi* arranged under President Cleveland.

In 1902 Hay arranged with Sir Robert Bond,

Prime Minister of Newfoundland, a new reciprocity agreement. This, however, the Senate rejected, and the Cleveland agreement continued. Newfoundland, angry at the rejection of the proposed treaty, put every obstacle possible in the way of American fishermen and used methods which the Americans claimed to be contrary to the treaty terms. After long continued and rather acrimonious discussions, the matter was finally referred in 1909 to the Hague Court. As in the Bering Sea case, the court was asked not only to judge the facts but also to draw up an agreement for the future. Its decision, on the whole, favored Newfoundland, but this fact is of little moment compared with the likelihood that a dispute almost a century and a half old has at last been permanently settled.

None of these international disputes and settlements to the north, however, excited anything like the popular interest aroused by one which occurred in the south. The Spanish War made it abundantly evident that an isthmian canal between the Atlantic and the Pacific must be built. The arguments of naval strategy which Captain Mahan had long been urging had received striking demonstration in the long and roundabout voyage which the *Oregon* was obliged to take. The pressure of railroad rates on the trade of the country caused wide commercial support for a project expected to establish a water competition that would pull them down. The American people determined to dig a canal.

The first obstacle to such a project lay in the Clayton-Bulwer Treaty with Great Britain. That obstacle Blaine had attempted in vain to remove; in fact his bungling diplomacy had riveted it yet more closely by making Great Britain maintain it as a point of honor. To this subject Hay now devoted himself, and as he encountered no serious difficulties, a treaty was drawn up in 1900 practically as he wished it. It was not, however, popular in the United States. Hay preferred and arranged for a canal neutralized by international guarantee, on the same basis as the Suez Canal; but American public sentiment had come to insist on a canal controlled absolutely by the United States. The treaty was therefore rejected by the Senate, or rather was so amended as to prove unacceptable to Great Britain.

Hay believed that he had obtained what was most desirable as well as all that was possible, that the majority of the American people approved, and that he was beaten only because a treaty must be approved by two-thirds of the Senate. He therefore resigned. President McKinley, however, refused to accept his resignation, and he and Lord Pauncefote were soon at work again on the subject. In 1901 a new treaty was presented to the Senate. This began by abrogating the Clayton-Bulwer Treaty entirely and with it brushing away all restrictions upon the activity of the United States in Central America. It specifically permitted the United States to "maintain such military police along the canal as may be necessary to protect it against lawlessness and disorder." By interpreting this clause as allowing complete fortification, the United States has made itself the guardian of the canal. In return for the release from former obligations which Great Britain thus allowed, the United States agreed that any canal constructed should be regulated by certain rules which were stated in the treaty and which made it "free and open to the vessels of commerce and of war of all nations observing these Rules, on terms of entire equality," in time of war as well as of peace. This time the treaty proved satisfactory and was accepted by the Senate. Thus one more source of trouble was done away with, and the first obstacle in the way of the canal was removed.

The Clayton-Bulwer Treaty was, however, only a bit of the tangled jungle which must be cleared before the first American shovel could begin its work. For over twenty years a contest had been waged between experts in the United States as to the relative merits of the Panama and the Nicaragua routes. The latter was the more popular, perhaps because it seemed at one time that Panama was preëmpted by De Lesseps' French company. This contest as to the better route led to the passage of a law, in 1902, which authorized the President to acquire the rights and property needed to construct a canal by the Panama route, on condition that he could make satisfactory arrangements "within a reasonable time and upon reasonable terms." Otherwise, Nicaragua was to be chosen. Theodore Roosevelt was now President and, though at one time not favoring Panama, he decided that there the canal should be constructed and with his accustomed vigor set himself to the task.

The first difficulty presented by this route was the prior right which the French company still retained, although it had little, if any, hope of carrying on the construction itself. It possessed not only rights but also much equipment on the spot, and it had actually begun excavation at certain points. The purchase of all its properties complete for $40,000,000 was, therefore, not a bad investment on the part of the Government. By this purchase the United States was brought directly into relation with Colombia, through one of whose federal states, Panama, the canal was to be cut.

While the French purchase had removed one obstacle, the De Lesseps charter alone would not suffice for the construction of the canal, for the American Government had definite ideas as to the conditions necessary for the success of the work. The Government required a zone which should be under its complete control, for not otherwise could satisfactory sanitary regulations be enforced. It insisted also on receiving the right to fortify the canal. It must have these and other privileges on a long time grant. For them, it was willing to pay generously. Negotiations would be affected, one could not say how, by the Treaty of 1846 with Colombia,[1] by which the United States had received the right of free use of the isthmus, with the right of maintaining the neutrality of the district and in return had guaranteed to Colombia sovereignty over the isthmus.

Hay took up the negotiations with the Colombian

[1] Then known as the Republic of New Granada.

*chargé d'affaires,* Dr. Herran, and arranged a treaty, which gave the United States a strip of land six miles wide across the isthmus, on a ninety-nine year lease, for which it should pay ten million dollars and, after a period of nine years for construction, a quarter of a million a year. This treaty, after months of debate in press and Congress, was rejected by the Colombian Senate on August 12 1903, though the people of Panama, nervously anxious lest this opportunity to sit on the bank of the world's great highway should slip into the hands of their rivals of Nicaragua, had urged earnestly the acceptance of the terms. The majority of the Colombians probably expected to grant the American requests in time but were determined to force the last penny from the United States. As Hay wrote: "The Isthmus is looked upon as a financial cow to be milked for the benefit of the country at large. This difficulty might be overcome by diplomacy and money."

President Roosevelt at this point took the negotiations into his own hands. Knowing that the price offered was more than just, he decided to depend no longer on bartering. He ordered the American minister to leave Colombia, and he prepared a message to Congress proposing that the

Americans proceed to dig the canal under authority which he claimed to find in the Treaty of 1846. It was, however, doubtful if Congress would find it there, particularly as so many Congressmen preferred the Nicaragua route. The President therefore listened with pleased attention to the rumors of a revolution planned to separate Panama from Colombia. Most picturesquely this information was brought by M. Philippe Bunau-Varilla, a former engineer of the De Lesseps company, who glowed with the excitement of coming events. Roosevelt, however, relied more upon the information furnished by two American officers, who reported "that various revolutionary movements were being inaugurated."

On October 10, 1903, the President wrote to Dr. Albert Shaw, of the *Review of Reviews:*

I enclose you, purely for your own information, a copy of a letter of September 5th, from our minister to Colombia. I think it might interest you to see that there was absolutely not the slightest chance of securing by treaty any more than we endeavored to secure. The alternatives were to go to Nicaragua against the advice of the great majority of competent engineers — some of the most competent saying that we had better have no canal at this time than go there — or else to take the territory by force without any attempt at getting a treaty. I cast aside the proposition made at the time to foment the secession of Panama. Whatever other governments can do, the United States cannot go into the securing, by such underhand means, the cession. Privately, I freely say to you that I should be delighted if Panama were an independent state; or if it made itself so at this moment; but for me to say so publicly would amount to an instigation of a revolt, and therefore I cannot say it.

Nothing, however, prevented the President from keeping an attentive eye on the situation. On the 16th of October he directed the Navy Department to send ships to the Isthmus to protect American interests in case of a revolutionary outbreak. On the 2d of November, he ordered the squadron to "maintain free and uninterrupted transit. . . . Prevent the landing of any armed force with hostile intent, either government or insurgent, at any point within fifty miles of Panama." At 3:40 P.M., on the 3d of November, the acting Secretary of State telegraphed to the Isthmus for confirmation of a report to the effect that an uprising was in progress. A reply dated 8:15 P.M. stated that there had been none as yet, but that it was rumored one would take place during the night. On the 4th of November independence was proclaimed. The only fatality was a Chinaman killed in the City of Panama by a shell from the Colombian gunboat *Bogota*. Its commander was warned not to fire again. On the 6th of November, Secretary Hay instructed our consul to recognize the new republic, and on the 13th of November, President Roosevelt received Bunau-Varilla as its representative at Washington.

This prompt recognition of a new state, without waiting to allow the parent Government time to assert itself, was contrary to American practice. The United States had regarded as a most unfriendly act Great Britain's mere recognition of the belligerency of the Southern Confederacy. The right of the United States to preserve the neutrality of the isthmus, as provided by the Treaty of 1846, certainly did not involve the right to intervene between the Government and revolutionists. On the other hand, the guarantee of possession which the United States had given to Colombia did involve supporting her Government to a reasonable extent; yet there could be little doubt that it was the presence of American ships which had made the revolution successful.

The possible implications of these glaring facts were cleverly met by President Roosevelt in his message to Congress and by the Secretary of State in the correspondence growing out of the affair. The Government really relied for its justification, however, not upon these technical pleas but upon the broad grounds of equity. America has learned in the last few years how important it is for its safety that "scraps of paper" be held sacred and how dangerous is the doctrine of necessity. Nevertheless it is well to observe that if the United States did, in the case of Panama, depart somewhat from that strict observance of obligations which it has been accustomed to maintain, it did not seek any object which was not just as useful to the world at large as to itself, that the situation had been created not by a conflict of opposing interests but by what the Government had good reason to believe was the bad faith of Colombia, and that the separation of Panama was the act of its own people, justly incensed at the disregard of their interests by their compatriots. This revolution created no tyrannized subject population but rather liberated from a galling bond a people who had, in fact, long desired separation.

With the new republic negotiation went on pleasantly and rapidly, and as early as November 18, 1903, a convention was drawn up, in which the United States guaranteed the independence of

Panama and in return received in perpetuity a grant of a zone ten miles wide within which to construct a canal from ocean to ocean.

# CHAPTER XVI

## PROBLEMS OF THE CARIBBEAN

As the acquisition of the Philippines made all Far Eastern questions of importance to the United States, so the investment of American millions in a canal across the Isthmus of Panama increased popular interest in the problems of the Caribbean. That fascinating sheet of water, about six hundred miles from north to south by about fifteen hundred from east to west, is ringed around by the possessions of many powers. In 1898 its mainland shores were occupied by Mexico, British Honduras, Guatemala, Honduras, Nicaragua, Costa Rica, Colombia, and Venezuela; its islands were possessed by the negro states of Hayti and the Dominican Republic, and by Spain, France, Great Britain, Holland, and Denmark. In the Caribbean had been fought some of the greatest and most significant naval battles of the eighteenth century and, when the canal was opened, across its waters would plough a great share of the commerce of the world. As owner of the canal and professed guardian of its use, the United States was bound to consider its own strategic relation to this sea into which the canal opened.

Gradually the situation which existed in 1898 has changed. Spain has been removed from the Caribbean. Of her former possessions the United States holds Porto Rico; Cuba is independent, but is in a way under the protection of the United States, which possesses on her coast the naval station of Guantánamo. The American treaty with the new republic of Panama practically created another American protectorate, and the fortification of the canal gave the United States another strategic position. The negotiation for the purchase of the Danish islands has been completed successfully. But these obvious footholds are of less importance than the more indirect relationships which the United States has been steadily establishing, through successive Administrations, with the various other powers located on the borders of the Caribbean.

The Spanish War did not lull the suspicions of the United States regarding the dangerous influence which would be exerted should the ambitions of European powers be allowed a field of action in the American continents, and the United States remained as intent as ever on preventing any opportunity for their gaining admittance. One such contingency, though perhaps a remote one, was the possibility of a rival canal, for there are other isthmuses than that of Panama which might be pierced with the aid of modern resources of capital and genius. To prevent any such action was not selfish on the part of the United States, for the American canal was to have an open door, and there was no economic justification for another seaway from the Atlantic to the Pacific.

There might, however, be some temptation in the political and military influence which such a prospective second canal could exert. Negotiations were begun, therefore, with all the transcontinental powers of Central America, offering liberal compensation for the control of all possible canal routes. These negotiations have been long drawn out and are only lately coming to fruition. They have served, however, to taboo all projects by other nations, and one of these treaties negotiated with Colombia, but not yet ratified, holds out the prospect of winning back her friendship which was so seriously alienated by the recognition of the republic of Panama by the United States.

In one respect the changing world has rendered quite obsolete the pronouncements of President Monroe. In the case of Japan there has grown up a great power which is neither European nor American. American policy in the Far East has made it abundantly evident that the United States does not regard the self-imposed limitations upon its ac-... .., .. extending to Asia. In her case there is lacking the *quid pro quo* by which the United States has justified its demand that European powers refrain from interfering in America. By no means, however, has the Government admitted the right of Asia to impinge on the American continents.

In 1912 Washington heard that Japan was negotiating with Mexico for a concession on Magdalena Bay. Senator Lodge promptly introduced a resolution in the Senate, declaring that "when any harbor or other place in the American continents is so situated that the occupation thereof for naval or military purposes might threaten the communication or the safety of the United States, the Government of the United States could not see, without grave concern, the possession of such harbor or other place by any corporation or association which has such relation to another government, not American, as to give that government practical

power of control for naval or military purposes."
This resolution, which passed the Senate by a
vote of 51 to 4, undoubtedly represented American sentiment, at least with regard to the foreign occupation of any territory bordering on
the Caribbean or on the Pacific between Panama
and California.

A more subtle danger lay in the financial claims
of European powers against the various states in
Central America, and the possibility of these claims
being used as levers to establish permanent control. Most of these foreign demands had a basis
in justice but had been exaggerated in amount.
They were of two kinds: first, for damage to
persons or property resulting from the numerous
revolutions and perpetual brigandage which have
scourged these semitropic territories; second, for
debts contracted in the name of the several countries for the most part to conduct revolutions or
to gild the after-career of defeated rulers in Paris,
— debts with a face value far in excess of the
amount received by the debtor and with accu-
mulated interest in many cases far beyond the
capacity of the several countries to pay. The
disputes as to the validity of such claims have been
without end, and they have furnished a constant

temptation to the cupidity of individuals and the ambition of the powers.

In 1902 Germany induced Great Britain and Italy to join her in an attempt to collect the amount of some of these claims from Venezuela. A joint squadron undertook a "pacific blockade" of the coast. Secretary Hay denied that a "pacific blockade" existed in international law and urged that the matter be submitted to arbitration. Great Britain and Italy were willing to come to an understanding and withdrew; but Germany, probably intent on ulterior objects, was unwilling and preferred to take temporary possession of certain ports. President Roosevelt then summoned the German Ambassador, Dr. Holleben, and told him that, unless Germany consented to arbitrate, Admiral Dewey would be ordered at noon ten days later to proceed to Venezuela and protect its coast. A week passed with no message. Holleben called on the President but rose to go without mentioning Venezuela. President Roosevelt thereupon informed the Ambassador that he had changed his mind and had decided to send Admiral Dewey one day earlier than originally planned; he further explained that in the event the Kaiser should decide to arbitrate, as not a word had been put on paper, there would be nothing to indicate coercion. Within thirty-six hours Holleben reported that Germany would arbitrate. Only once before, when Seward was dealing with Napoleon III concerning Mexico, had forcible persuasion been used to maintain the Monroe Doctrine.

It was perfectly clear that if the United States sat idly by and allowed European powers to do what they would to collect their Latin American debts, the Monroe Doctrine would soon become a dead letter. It was not, however, so plain how American interference could be justified. The problem was obviously a difficult one and did not concern the United States alone. Latin America was even more vitally concerned with it, and her statesmen, always lucid exponents of international law, were active in devising remedies. Carlos Calvo of Argentina advanced the doctrine that "the collection of pecuniary claims made by the citizens of one country against the government of another country should never be made by force." Señor Drago, Minister of Foreign Affairs in the same country in 1902, urged upon the United States a modification of the same view by asserting that "the public debt cannot occasion armed intervention."

President Roosevelt handled the matter in his messages of 1903 and 1904. "That our rights and interests are deeply concerned in the maintenance of the [Monroe] Doctrine is so clear as hardly to need argument. This is especially true in view of the construction of the Panama Canal. As a mere matter of self defense we must exercise a close watch over the approaches to this canal, and this means we must be thoroughly alive to our interests in the Caribbean Sea." "When we announce a policy . . . we thereby commit ourselves to the consequences of the policy." "Chronic wrong-doing or an impotence which results in a general loosening of the ties of civilized society, may in America, as elsewhere, ultimately require inter-vention by some civilized nation, and in the West-ern Hemisphere the adherence of the United States to the Monroe Doctrine may force the United States, however reluctantly. in flagrant cases of such wrongdoing or impotence to the exercise of an international police power.'

To prevent European intervention for the pur-pose of securing just claims in America, then, the United States would undertake to handle the case, and would wield the "Big Stick" against any American state which should refuse to meet its obligations. This was a repetition, in a different tone, of Blaine's "Elder Sister" program. As developed, it had elements also of Cleveland's Venezuela policy. In 1907 the United States submitted to the Hague Conference a modified form of the Drago doctrine, which stated that the use of force to collect contract debts claimed from one government by another as being due to its citizens should be regarded as illegal, unless the creditor nation offered to submit its claims to arbitration and this offer were refused by the nation against which the claim was directed. The interference of the United States, therefore, would be practically to hale the debtor into court.

Around the Caribbean, however, were several nations not only unwilling but unable to pay their debts. This inability was not due to the fact that national resources were lacking, but that constant revolution scared away conservative capital from seeking constructive investment or from developing their natural riches, while speculators loaned money at ruinous rates of discount to tottering presidents, gambling on the possibility of some turn in fortune that would return them tenfold. The worst example of an insolvent and recalcitrant state was the Dominican Republic, whose superb harbors were a constant temptation to ambitious powers willing to assume its debts in return for naval stations, and whose unscrupulous rulers could nearly always be bribed to sell their country as readily as anything else. In the case of this country President Roosevelt made a still further extension of the Monroe Doctrine when, in 1905, he concluded a treaty whereby the United States agreed to undertake the adjustment of the republic's obligations and the administration of its custom houses, and at the same time guarantee the territorial integrity of the republic. This arrangement was hotly attacked in the United States as an indication of growing imperialism, and, though it was defended as necessary to prevent the entrance of new foreign influences into the Caribbean, the opposition was so strong that the treaty was not accepted by the Senate until 1907, and then only in a modified form with the omission of the territorial guarantee.

For the United States thus to step into a foreign country as an administrator was indeed a startling innovation. On the other hand, the development of such a policy was a logical sequence of the Monroe Doctrine. That it was a step in the general development of policy on the part of the United

States and not a random leap is indicated by the manner in which it has been followed up. In 1911 treaties with Nicaragua and Honduras somewhat similar to the Dominican protocol were negotiated by Secretary Knox but failed of ratification. Subsequently under President Wilson's Administration, the treaty with Nicaragua was redrafted and was ratified by both parties. Hayti, too, was in financial difficulties and, at about the time of the outbreak of the Great War, it was reported that Germany was about to relieve her needs at the price of harbors and of control. In 1915, however, the United States took the island under its protection by a treaty which not only gave the Government complete control of the fiscal administration but bound it to "lend an efficient aid for the preservation of Haitian independence and the maintenance of a government adequate for the protection of life, property, and individual liberty."

Since 1898, then, the map of the Caribbean has completely changed its aspect. The sea is not an American lake, nor do the Americans wish it to be such. In time, as the surrounding countries become better able to stand alone, direct interference on the part of the United States will doubtless become less than it is today. There is, however, practically no present opportunity for a non-American power to establish itself and to threaten the commerce or the canal of the United States.

Few people in the United States and perhaps fewer in the countries involved realize from what American influence has saved these small states. A glance at Africa and Asia will suggest what would otherwise have been the case. Without the United States and its leadership, there can be little doubt that giant semisovereign corporations owing allegiance to some great power would now possess these countries. They would bristle with forts and police, and their populations would be in a state of absolute political and of quasi-economic servitude. They might today be more orderly and perhaps wealthier, but unless the fundamental American belief in democracy and self-government is wrong they would be infinitely farther from their true goal, which involves the working out of their own civilization.

The Caribbean is but a portion of the whole international problem of the Americas, and the methods used by the United States in solving its problems seemed likely to postpone that sympathetic union of the whole to which it has been looking forward for a century. Yet this country has not been unappreciative of the larger aspects of Pan-Americanism. In 1899 President McKinley revived Blaine's project and proposed a Pan-American congress. To popularize this idea, a Pan-American Exposition was arranged at Buffalo in 1901. Here, just after he had expounded his views of the ties that might bind the continents together, McKinley was assassinated. The idea, however, lived and in the same year a congress was held at the City of Mexico, where it was proposed that such meetings be held regularly. As a result, congresses were held at Rio de Janeiro in 1906 and at Buenos Aires in 1910, at which various measures of common utility were discussed and a number of projects were actually undertaken.

The movement of Pan-Americanism has missed achieving the full hopes of its supporters owing not so much to a difference of fundamental ideas and interests as to suspicion and national pride. The chief powers of southern South America — Argentina, Brazil, and Chili — had by the end of the nineteenth century in large measure successfully worked out their own problems. They resented the interference of a power of alien race such as the United States, and they suspected its good intentions in wielding the "Big Stick," especially after the cavalier treatment which Colombia had received.

They observed with alarm the strengthening of the grip of the United States about the Caribbean. United in a group, known from their initials as the "A. B. C." powers, they sought to assume the leadership of Latin America, basing their action, indeed, upon the fundamentals of the Monroe Doctrine — the exclusion of foreign influence and the independence of peoples — but with themselves instead of the United States as chief guardians.

Many of the publicists of these three powers, however, doubted their capacity to walk entirely alone. On the one hand they noted the growing influence of the Germans in Brazil and the indications of Japanese interest in many places, and on the other they divined the fundamental sincerity of the professions of the United States and were anxious to coöperate with this nation. Not strong enough to control the policy of the various countries, these men at least countered those chauvinists who urged that hostility to the United States was a first duty compared with which the danger of non-American interference might be neglected.

Confronted by this divided attitude, the United States sought to win over but not to compel. Nothing more completely met American views than that each power should maintain for itself the principles of the Monroe Doctrine by excluding foreign influences. Beyond that the United States sought only friendship, and, if it were agreeable, such unity as should be mutually advantageous. In 1906 Elihu Root, the Secretary of State, made a tour of South America with a view of expressing these sentiments; and in 1913–1914 ex-Pres ent Roosevelt took occasion, on the way to his Br il-ian hunting trip, to assure the people of the gi t South American powers that the "Big Stick" w s not intended to intimidate them. Pan-America n unity was still, when President Taft went out cf office in 1913, an aspiration rather than a realized fact, though the tangible evidences of unity had vastly multiplied since 1898, and the recurring congresses provided a basis of organization upon which some substantial structure might be built.

The United States had sincerely hoped that Mexico, like the "A. B. C." powers, was another Latin American power which had found itself. Of all it was certainly the most friendly and the most intimate. The closeness of its relations with the United States is indicated by the fact that in the forty years between 1868 and 1908, forty agree-ments, treaties, and conventions had been con-cluded between the two countries. Nor was intimacy confined to the Governments. The peace arranged by President Diaz had brought foreign capital by the billion to aid the internal development of the country, and of this money more had come from the United States than from any other nation. Nor was it financial aid alone which had gone across the border. There was but little American colonization, it is true, but business managers, engineers, mine foremen, and ranch superintendents formed thousands of links binding the nations together. The climax of intimacy seemed reached when, in 1910, a general treaty of arbitration was made after President Taft and President Diaz had met at El Paso on the Mexican border in a personal conference. A personal interview between the President of the United States and the chief of a foreign state was almost unique in American history, owing to the convention that the President should not depart from the national territory.

It was, therefore, with a bitter sense of disappointment that Americans heard of the revolution inaugurated in 1910 by Francisco Madero. In common with France, Spain, Great Britain, and Germany, the United States was disturbed for the safety of the investments and persons of its citizens.   The Government was also concerned because the points of first and most persistent fighting were where the various railroads crossed the American boundary.   This circumstance brought the whole border within the range of disturbance. The Government was apprehensive, too, as to the effect of long-continued war upon territories within the circle of its chief interest, the Caribbean ᴄ. ᴀ. Yet, when the first surprise caused by the revolution had passed and the reason for the outbreak was perceived, — the fact that the order and apparent prosperity of the Diaz régime had been founded upon the oppression and exploitation of the masses, — public sympathy in the United States went out to Madero and his supporters.

The Diaz Government collapsed with surprising suddenness.   The resignation of President Diaz in May, 1911, was accepted as a proof of the popular character and the success of the revolution, and Madero, who was elected president in October, was promptly recognized as the constitutional head of the Mexican Government.   The revolution, however, aroused the United States to the fact that there still persisted the era of disturbance which it had hoped was drawing to a close in Latin America.   With this disturbing revelation in mind,

Congress took another step in the development of American policies consequent upon the Monroe Doctrine by passing an act authorizing the President, whenever he should "find that in any American country conditions of domestic violence exist which are promoted by the use of arms and munitions of war procured from the United States," to prohibit trade in such articles. Under this authority, President Taft promptly forbade the export of such articles to Mexico except to the Government.

Real revolutions, however, seldom result simply in the transfer of authority from one group to another. The breaking of the bonds of recognized authority releases all sorts of desires, represented in the state by separate groups, each of which sees no reason for accepting the control of another. All seek to seize the dropped reins. The inauguration of Madero, therefore, did not result in a new and popular government but in continued disturbance. Factions with differing creeds raised revolts in various sections of the country until, in February, 1913, Madero was overthrown by one of these groups, led by Felix Diaz and General Victoriano Huerta, and representing a reactionary tendency. Madero and his vice president Pino Suarez were killed, it was believed by order of Huerta, and on the 27th of February, in the City of Mexico, Huerta was proclaimed President. Don Venustiano Carranza, Governor of the State of Coahuila, straightway denied the constitutionality of the new Government and led a new revolution under the banner of the Constitution.

It was in such a condition that President Wilson found the affairs of the continent when he took office on March 4, 1913. The American policy in the Caribbean was well defined and to a large extent in operation. Pan-American sentiment was developing, but its strength and direction were yet to be determined. Mexico was in chaos, and upon the Government's handling of it would depend the final success of the United States in the Caribbean and the possibility of effecting a real and fruitful coöperation of the Americas.

# CHAPTER XVII

## WORLD RELATIONSHIPS

IT became increasingly evident that the foreign policy of the United States could not consist solely of a Caribbean policy, a Pan-American policy, and a Far Eastern policy, but that it must necessarily involve a world policy. During the years after the Spanish War the world was actively discussing peace; but all the while war was in the air. The peace devices of 1815, the Holy and the Quadruple Alliances, had vanished. The world had ceased to regard buffer states as preventives of wars between the great nations, although at the time few believed that any nation would ever dare to treat them as Germany since then has treated Belgium. The balance of power still existed, but statesmen were ever uncertain as to whether such a relation of states was really conducive to peace or to war. A concert of the Great Powers resembling the Quadruple Alliance sought to regulate

uch vexing problems as were presented by the
Balkans and China, but their concord was not
oud enough to drown the notes of discord.

The outspoken word of governments was still all
or peace; their proposals for preserving it were
f two kinds. First, there was the time-honored
rgument that the best preservative of peace was
reparation for war. Foremost in the avowed poli-
ies of the day, this was urged by some who really
elieved it, by ome who hoped for war and in-
ended to be read for it, and by the cynical who
id not wish for war but thought it inevitable. The
ther proposal was that war could and should be
prevented by agreements to submit all differences
between nations to international tribunals for judgment. In the United States, which had always
rejected the idea of balance of power, and which
only in Asia, and to a limited degree, assented to
the concert of powers, one or the other of these
two views was urged by all those who saw that the
United States had actually become a world power,
that isolation no longer existed, and that a policy of
nonintervention could not keep us permanently
detached from the current of world politics.

The foremost advocates of preparedness were
Theodore Roosevelt and Admiral Mahan. It was

little enough that they were able to accomplish
but it was more than most Americans realize. The
doubling of the regular army which the Spanish
War had brought about was maintained but was
less important than its improvement in organiza
tion. Elihu Root and William H. Taft, as Secre
taries of War, profiting by the lessons learned in
Cuba, established a general staff, provided for the
advanced professional training of officers, and be
came sufficiently acquainted with the personnel to
bring into positions of responsibility those who
deserved to hold them. The navy grew with less
resistance on the part of the public, which now was
interested in observing the advance in the rank of
its fleet among the navies of the world. When in
1907 Roosevelt sent the American battleship squadron on a voyage around the world, the expedition
not only caused a pleased self-consciousness at
home but perhaps impressed foreign nations with
the fact that the United States now counted not
only as a potential but as an actual factor in
world affairs.

Greater popular interest, if one may judge from
relative achievement, was aroused by the proposal to substitute legal for military battles. The
United States had always been disposed to submit

to arbitration questions which seemed deadlocked. The making of general arrangements for the arbitration of cases that might arise in the future was now advocated. The first important proposal of this character was made to the United States by Great Britain at the time of the Venezuela affair. This proposal was rejected, for it was regarded as a device of Great Britain to cover her retreat in that particular case by suggesting a general provision. The next suggestion was that made by the Czar, in 1899, for a peace conference at The Hague. This invitation the United States accepted with hearty good will and she concurred in the establishment of a permanent court of arbitration to meet in that city. Andrew Carnegie built a home for it, and President Roosevelt sent to it as its first case that of the "Pious Fund," concerning which the United States had long been in dispute with Mexico.

The establishment of a world court promoted the formation of treaties between nations by which they agreed to submit their differences to The Hague or to similar courts especially formed. A model, or as it was called a "mondial" treaty was drawn up by the conference for this purpose. Secretary Hay proceeded to draw up treaties on such general lines with a number of nations, and President Roosevelt referred them to the Senate with his warm approval. That body, however, exceedingly jealous of the share in the treaty-making power given it by the Constitution, disliked the treaties, because it feared that under such general agreements cases would be submitted to The Hague Court without its special approval.[1] Yet, as popular sentiment was strongly behind the movement the Senate ventured only to amend the procedure in such a way as to make every "agreement" treaty which would require its concurrence. President Roosevelt, however, was so much incensed at this important change that he refused to continue the negotiations.

President Taft was perhaps more interested in this problem than in any other. His Secretary of State, Elihu Root, reopened negotiations and, in 1908 and 1909, drew up a large number of treaties in a form which met the wishes of the Senate. Before the Administration closed, the United States had agreed to submit to arbitration all questions, except those of certain classes especially

[1] The second article in these treaties read: "In each individual case the high contracting parties, before appealing to the Permanent Court of Arbitration, shall conclude a special agreement defining clearly the matter in dispute."

reserved, that might arise with Great Britain, France, Austro-Hungary, China, Costa Rica, Italy, Denmark, Japan, Hayti, Mexico, the Netherlands, Norway, Paraguay, Spain, Sweden, Peru, San Salvador, and Switzerland.

Such treaties seemed to a few fearsome souls to be violations of the injunctions of Washington and Jefferson to avoid entangling alliances, but to most they seemed, rather, to be disentangling. It was, indeed, becoming increasingly apparent that the world was daily growing smaller and that, as its parts were brought together by rail and steamships, by telegraph and wireless, more and more objects of common interest must become subject to common regulation. General Grant can hardly be regarded as a visionary, and yet in 1873 in his second inaugural address, he had said: "Commerce, education, and rapid transit of thought and matter by telegraph and steam have changed all this. . . . I believe that our Great Maker is preparing the world in His own good time, to become one nation, speaking one language, and when armies and navies will be no longer required."

Quietly, without general interest, or even particular motive, the United States had accepted its share in handling many such world problems. As early as 1875 it had coöperated in founding and maintaining at Paris an International Bureau of Weights and Measures. In 1886 it joined in an international agreement for the protection of submarine cables; in 1890, in an agreement for the suppression of the African slave trade; in 1899, in an agreement for the regulation of the importation of spirituous liquors into Africa; in 1902, in a convention of American powers for the Arbitration of Pecuniary Claims. In 1903 it united with various American powers in an International Sanitary Convention; in 1905 it joined with most countries of the world in establishing and maintaining an International Institute of Agriculture at Rome. It would surprise most Americans to know that five hundred pages of their collection of *Treaties and Conventions* consist of such international undertakings, which amount in fact to a body of international legislation. It is obvious that the Government, in interpreting the injunction to avoid entangling alliances, has not found therein prohibition against international coöperation.

In 1783 the United States had been a little nation with not sufficient inhabitants to fill up its million square miles of territory. Even in 1814 it still reached only to the Rockies and still found a troublesome neighbor lying between it and the Gulf of Mexico. Now with the dawn of the twentieth century it was a power of imperial dimensions, occupying three million square miles between the Atlantic and the Pacific, controlling the Caribbean, and stretching its possessions across the Pacific and up into the Arctic. Its influence was a potent factor in the development of Asia, and it was bound by the bonds of treaties, which it has ever regarded sacred, to assist in the regulation of many matters of world interest.

Nor had the only change during the century been that visible in the United States. The world which seemed so vast and mysterious in 1812 had opened up most of its dark places to the valor of adventurous explorers, of whom the United States had contributed its fair share. The facilities of intercourse had conquered space, and along with its conquest had gone a penetration of the countries of the world by the tourist and the immigrant, the missionary and the trader, so that Terence's statement that nothing human was alien to him had become perforce true of the world.

Nor had the development of governmental organization stood still. In 1812 the United States was practically the only democratic republic in the world; in 1912 the belief in a government founded on the consent of the governed, and republican in form, had spread over all the Americas, except such portions as were still colonies, and was practically true of even most of them. Republican institutions had been adopted by France and Portugal, and the spirit of democracy had permeated Great Britain and Norway and was gaining yearly victories elsewhere. In 1912 the giant bulk of China adopted the form of government commended to her by the experience of the nation which, more than any other, had preserved her integrity. Autocracy and divine right, however, were by no means dead. On the contrary, girt and prepared, they were arming themselves for a final stand. But no longer, as in 1823, was America pitted alone against Europe. It was the world including America which was now divided against itself.

It was chiefly the Spanish War which caused the American people slowly and reluctantly to realize this new state of things — that the ocean was no longer a barrier in a political or military sense, and that the fate of each nation was irrevocably bound up with the fate of all. As the years went by, however, Americans came to see that the isolation proclaimed by President Monroe was no longer real, and that isolation even as a tradition could not, either for good or for ill, long endure. All thoughtful men saw that a new era needed a new policy; the wiser, however, were not willing to give up all that they had acquired in the experience of the past. They remembered that the separation of the continents was not proclaimed as an end in itself but as a means of securing American purposes. Those national purposes had been: first, the securing of the right of self-government on the part of the United States; second, the securing of the right of other nations to govern themselves. Both of these aims rested on the belief that one nation should not interfere with the domestic affairs of another. These fundamental American purposes remained, but it was plain that the situation would force the nation to find some different method of realizing them. The action of the United States indicated that the hopes of the people ran to the reorganization of the world in such a way as would substitute the arbitrament of courts for that of war. Year by year the nation committed itself more strongly to coöperation foreshadowing such an organization. While this feeling was growing among the people, the number of those who doubted whether such a system could ward off war altogether and forever also increased. Looking forward to the probability of war, they could not fail to fear that the next would prove a world war, and that in the event of such a conflict, the non-interference of the United States would not suffice to preserve it immune in any real independence.

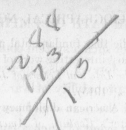

# BIBLIOGRAPHICAL NOTE

EACH President's *Annual Message* always gives a brief survey of the international relations of the year and often makes suggestions of future policy. Of these the most famous is Monroe's message in 1823. Since 1860 they have been accompanied by a volume of *Foreign Relations*, giving such correspondence as can be made public at the time. The full correspondence of particular cases is sometimes called for by the Congress, in which case it is found in the *Executive Documents* of House or Senate. A fairly adequate selection of all such papers before 1828 is found in *American State Papers, Foreign Affairs*. Three volumes contain the American *Treaties, Conventions, International Acts*, etc., to 1913. A. B. Hart's *Foundations of American Foreign Policy* (1901) gives a good bibliography of these and other sources.

More intimate material is found in the lives and works of diplomats, American and foreign. Almost all leave some record, but there are unfortunately fewer of value since 1830 than before that date. The *Memoirs* of John Quincy Adams (1874–1877), and his *Writings*, (1913– ), are full of fire and information, and W. C. Ford, in his *John Quincy Adams and the Monroe Doctrine*, in the *American Historical Review*, vol. VII, pp. 676–696, and vol. VIII, pp. 28–52, enables us to sit at the council table while that fundamental policy was being evolved. The most interesting work of this kind for the later period is *The Life and Letters of John Hay*, by W. R. Thayer, 2 vols. (1915).

Treatments of American diplomacy as a whole are few. J. W. Foster's *Century of American Diplomacy* (1901) ends with 1876. C. R. Fish in *American Diplomacy* (1915) gives a narrative from the beginning to the present time. W. A. Dunning's *The British Empire and the United States* (1914) is illuminating and interesting. Few countries possess so firm a basis for the understanding of their relations with the world as J. B. Moore has laid down in his *Digest of International Law*, 8 vols. (1906), and his *History and Digest of International Arbitrations*, 6 vols. (1898).

Particular episodes and subjects have attracted much more the attention of students. Of the library of works on the Monroe Doctrine, A. B. Hart's *The Monroe Doctrine, an Interpretation* (1916) can be most safely recommended. On the Clayton-Bulwer Treaty, M. W. Williams's *Anglo-American Isthmian Diplomacy, 1815–1915* (1916) combines scholarly accuracy with interest. A. R. Colquhoun's *The Mastery of the Pacific* (1902) has sweep; and no one will regret reading R. L. Stevenson's *A Footnote to History* (1892), though it deals but with the toy kingdom of Samoa.

The most important history of the Spanish War is Admiral F. E. Chadwick's *The Relations of the United States and Spain*, one volume of which, *Diplomacy* (1909), deals with the long course of relations which explain the war; and two volumes, *Spanish-American War* (1911), give a narrative and critical account of the war itself. E. J. Benton's *International Law and Diplomacy of the*

*Spanish-American War* (1908) is a good review of the particular aspects indicated in the title. The activity of the navy is discussed from various angles by J. D. Long, *The New American Navy*, 2 vols. (1903), and by H. H. Sargent in *The Campaign of Santiago de Cuba*, 3 vols. (1907), in which he gives a very valuable documentary and critical history of the chief campaign. General Joseph Wheeler has told the story from the military point of view in *The Santiago Campaign* (1899), and Theodore Roosevelt in *The Rough Riders* (1899). A good military account of the whole campaign is H. W. Wilson's *The Downfall of Spain* (1900). Russell A. Alger in *The Spanish-American War* (1901) attempts to defend his administration of the War Department. General Frederick Funston, in his *Memories of Two Wars* (1911) proves himself as interesting as a writer as he was picturesque as a fighter. J. A. LeRoy, in *The Americans in the Philippines*, 2 vols. (1914), gives a very careful study of events in those islands to the outbreak of guerrilla warfare. C. B. Elliott's *The Philippines*, 2 vols. (1917), is an excellent study of American policy and its working up to the Wilson Administration. W. F. Willoughby discusses governmental problems in his *Territories and Dependencies of the United States* (1905).

On the period subsequent to the Spanish War, J. H. Latané's *America as a World Power* (in the *American Nation Series*, 1907) is excellent. A. C. Coolidge's *The United States as a World Power* (1908) is based on a profound understanding of European as well as American conditions. C. L. Jones's *Caribbean Interests of the United States* (1916) is a comprehensive survey. The *Autobiography of Theodore Roosevelt* (1913) is indispensable for an understanding of the spirit of his Administration. W.

H. Taft's *The United States and Peace* (1914) is a source, a history, and an argument.

The *International Year Book* and the *American Year Book* contain annual accounts written by men of wide information and with great attention to accuracy. Such periodic treatments, however, are intended to be, and are, valuable for fact rather than for interpretation.

# INDEX

20